A BIT BE

NEW YORK   TORONTO   SYDNEY   HOLLYWOOD

465463819

MADE AND PRINTED IN GREAT BRITAIN BY
LATIMER TREND & COMPANY LTD PLYMOUTH

MADE IN ENGLAND

A BIT BETWEEN THE TEETH

First presented by the Brian Rix *Theatre of Laughter*, in association with Pieter Toerien and the Yvonne Arnaud Theatre, and by arrangement with Larry Parnes at the Cambridge Theatre, London, on September 12th, 1974, with the following cast of characters:

Fogg	Brian Rix
Ruff	Peter Bland
Reaper	Jimmy Logan
Diane Reaper	Donna Reading
Mrs Barker	Vivienne Johnson

The Play directed by Wallace Douglas
Setting by Brian Currah

ACT I The flat above Reaper & Fogg, Jewellers, London. One evening
ACT II Immediately following

Time—the present
Weather—English

ACT I

Roger Fogg's attic flat in London. Early evening, about 7 p.m.

It is a combined set, comprising a small kitchen, a sitting-room and a bed-room. In the kitchen is an electric stove with four hotplates, which glow red when switched on. Beside it is a section of working-top, above which is a practical window which, when opened, gives a view of rooftops. Immediately above the electric stove is a swivel-hanger used for drying dishcloths. There is also a sink with practical taps: below it is a cupboard in which is a waste-bin. Along one wall is a working-top into which is built a refrigerator (not practical). There is also a broom cupboard large enough to house a person. In the sitting-room there are two doors. The first is presumed to lead down to the jeweller's shop below—it is referred to as the shop door. The second is presumed to lead down to the lower front door and is referred to as the front door. At the back is another door connecting the sitting-room to the bedroom. In the sitting-room are a sofa, a drinks table and an easy chair with low back: near the kitchen door, in the sitting-room, is a table or built-in fitment containing a drawer, and on top of this is a telephone. On the wall near the front door is an intercom for remote control of the front door below. Below the connecting door to the bedroom, and above the sofa, is a complicated-looking board which is the burglar alarm control. In the bedroom is a red burglar alarm bell near the connecting door. In the back wall is a window with a practical sash, which looks out on to the rooftops: it has long curtains covering it. There is a door from the bedroom to the bathroom, of which only a wall with a shelf can be seen. Below the connecting door is a table on which is a lamp with twin circular glass shades. There is a built-in wardrobe with sliding-doors, and also a single bed with head against the wall. (See the plan of the set and the Furniture Plot, page 64)

The CURTAIN *rises to the sound of heavy rain. The Lights are on in the living-room and kitchen. Suddenly the alarm bell starts ringing. There is a sound of someone running upstairs, and Roger Fogg enters through the front door, carrying a small tin of baked beans, two pies and a dripping um-brella. Fogg is a pleasant, slightly pompous fellow, who is probably brilliant at his job, but unworldly about women and apt to panic in a crisis. He wears a very respectable black jacket and grey pinstripe trousers. He hangs the umbrella up near the telephone and puts down the pies and beans. He picks up an instruction pamphlet from the top of the burglar alarm*

Fogg (*reading aloud*) "To disconnect the burglar alarm turn up Switch One." (*He does so*)

Immediately a loud buzzer goes off. He switches it off. He looks at the instructions and peers closely at the board. He turns the instructions upside down and looks at the board again. This seems to do no good. He starts to count the switches and ends up pointing at the switch which is on the bottom row at the far right

Five-four-three-two-one. Japanese! (*He consults the instructions again, holding them in one hand and experimenting with the other*) Two—ultrasonic protection.

A high-pitched noise is heard. He switches it off

Three—under-carpet floor-pads. (*He turns the switch down and walks round the room testing the floor*)

Nothing happens. As he returns to the alarm the bell goes off. He switches it off

Four—exterior flood-lighting. (*He turns another switch down, then opens the connecting door, enters the bedroom, parts the window curtains and looks through. He nods to himself, satisfied, returns to the sitting-room and turns off Switch Four. He consults the instructions again*) Five—on/off warning buzzer. (*He turns on Switch Five*)

A nasty beeping buzzer sounds. He switches it off. From the direction of outside the bedroom window comes a definite noise. He freezes, cocking an ear. He turns out the sitting-room lights, crosses the sitting-room silently and enters the kitchen

Simultaneously, Ruff enters through the bedroom window, parting the curtains. His silent, shifty entrance gives the impression that he is a burglar. He is a thick-set fellow, wearing a sopping raincoat and trilby hat

In the kitchen Fogg picks up a rolling-pin and starts to make a return journey. Ruff approaches the connecting door from one side, and Fogg approaches it from the other. Simultaneously they both bend down and peek through the keyhole, and both evidently see nothing. As Fogg enters the bedroom Ruff presses himself back against the wall. Fogg walks into the bedroom and approaches the window with the rolling-pin at the ready. Ruff creeps up behind him and switches on the lights

Ruff Hold it, hold it! I wouldn't use that, son. Someone might get hurt.

Fogg turns, quaking

Fogg (*shakily*) Nothing worth stealing here. Nothing.
Ruff Good. Good. Checked that, did you? Drop that!

Fogg obediently drops the rolling-pin

(*Pleasantly*) There's a good lad. (*Advancing, smiling pleasantly*) Let's keep it nice and friendly, eh?

Fogg nods nervously. Ruff suddenly lams out and gives Fogg a mighty whack in the midriff, doubling him up and bringing him on to the bed. Ruff picks up the rolling-pin and puts it on the table near the door

Now then, what's your name?
Fogg Ooooo . . .! Aaaagh . . .! Urrrr . . .! Ooo . . .!
Ruff You going to answer proper or do I have to nudge you again?
Fogg Oooh! Agh! Take everything—but no violence, please.

Ruff I asked for your name, son.

Fogg Fogg. Roger Fogg.

Ruff (*reacting*) Fogg? Of Reaper and Fogg? The jeweller's shop down-stairs?

Fogg Yes, and I warn you you won't get away with this. The police will be on your tail the second you leave here.

Ruff (*somewhat embarrassed*) I am the police, sir. Inspector Ruff. (*He produces his card*)

Fogg Police? You struck me!

Ruff (*indicating the rolling-pin*) Self-defence, sir.

Fogg Self-defence! I didn't even know you were in here.

Ruff picks up the rolling-pin then puts it down again

Ruff You weren't making pastry with that, were you, sir?

Fogg Of course I wasn't.

Ruff There you are, then. And what were you doing, creeping about your own place in the dark?

Fogg I heard someone on the roof.

Ruff That was me, sir.

Fogg And what the dickens are you doing on my roof and breaking in here?

Ruff Didn't break in, sir. The window was open.

Fogg Don't prevaricate, man. I know my rights. Explain yourself and it had better be good.

Ruff Yes, sir. For various reasons I have a man posted on the roof two houses down from here. We had a tip-off that the Quiet Gang were going to do a job in this area tonight.

Fogg Oh? The diamond thieves?

Ruff Yes, and I saw something moving on the roof, so came to investigate.

Fogg What was it?

Ruff A small tabby cat and a large white cat in—er—conference. (*He shows his hand*) The white one scratched me. I think they resented being parted.

Fogg Oh! That's Sweetie. My cat. (*He goes to the window, which is still open, and calls outside*) Sweetie! Sweetie! Come here, you naughty puss. What are you doing in this rain—as if we didn't know. Come along—good puss . . .

Fogg reaches out of the window and reappears holding a cat (this can be an imitation cat)

Here we are. Bad thing. Now you go downstairs and chase those mice. (*He carries the cat through the connecting door, opens the shop door, and pushes the cat through. Then he closes the door and turns on the lights*)

Ruff follows Fogg into the sitting-room and eyes the burglar alarm controls

Ruff What on earth's that, sir?

Fogg (*proudly*) Control-board for the burglar alarm.

Ruff Whew! Complicated-looking thing.

Fogg It is. Latest from Japan. They only finished installing it today. Ooh. (*He rubs his stomach*)

Ruff Extremely sorry about that, sir. A case of mistaken identity. (*Looking hungrily at the drinks table*) Maybe a tot of brandy or whisky would do you good?

Fogg I never touch alcohol in any form.

Ruff Really? (*With emphasis*) Wish I could say the same.

Fogg And no doubt you don't drink on duty.

Ruff No, sir.

Fogg Well, if that's all ...?

Ruff gives the drinks another look, then turns his collar up

Ruff It looks like it. Brr! Pelting with rain, and freezing out. Real brandy weather.

Fogg That doesn't affect me. I'm not going out tonight.

Ruff You're lucky. Well, I'll be off. Here's hoping I meet a friendly St Bernard on my way. Ha! Ha!

Fogg makes no response

With my luck he'll probably bite me.

Fogg I'll take you down through the shop. If there is to be any trouble with the diamond thieves I'd better double check I've locked the door correctly.

Ruff I should put a lock on the whisky, too!

Ruff and Fogg exit through the shop door, leaving it open. After a brief pause Eddie Reaper enters through the front door. He is Fogg's partner—middleaged-ish, but dressed in the latest fashion and latest hair-style. He can be extremely charming, especially when it comes to women—to whom he dedicates a great deal of his time. He wears a coat and hat, and carries a dripping umbrella. He chews the tag end of a fat cigar. He draws vainly at this, then throws it into the wastepaper-basket. He takes off his coat and hangs it up, with the umbrella, near the front door

Reaper (*calling quietly*) Fogg! Foggy! Can I use your telephone? (*He notices the baked beans and picks them up*) Baked beans! Must be having an orgy! (*Somewhat surreptitiously, he approaches the phone and quickly dials a number*) Hullo? Di-Di? Is that you? . . . This is me. The car's parked in Smedley's yard as usual. I'll meet you at the gate in about ten minutes, but listen: as soon as we reach the car get into the back and lie flat on the floor. (*He listens, and reacts*) No, sweetheart, *not* the same as last time. *We're* not lying in the back. *You* are, alone. . . . I'll be in the front. . . . I just don't want anyone local to see you. . . . No. No. . . . Don't get upset! I'm only going to be in the front because I'll be driving. (*With an air of giving good news*) Yes! We're not staying in the yard this time. I've booked us into a hotel! Isn't that great? . . . Well, no—no. It isn't the Savoy, actually. It's the next best thing. It's a little place in Paddington, quite clean. . . . The Taj Mahal. And I'll bring a bottle of champagne.

Fogg (*off*) Sweetie?

Reaper Must go. 'Bye! (*He hangs up and hides by the front door*)

Fogg enters through the shop door

Fogg Sweetie? Sweetie? Where are you?

Reaper jumps out

Reaper I'm here, darling!

Fogg Aaaagh! (*He drops to his knees*) Oh, it's you, Eddie!

Reaper So, you're expecting a sweetie!

Fogg Oh, you gave me a fright. (*He rises, reacting*) Don't say my front door below was open?

Reaper No. Safely locked.

Fogg Then how on earth did you get in?

Reaper (*producing a key*) Used this key.

Fogg What are you doing with a key to my flat?

Reaper I'm your partner, aren't I? And it was my flat, remember.

Fogg It's mine, now; so what are you doing with a key to it?

Reaper I kept a spare in case of accidents.

Fogg What accidents?

Reaper We—ell. Suppose you gassed yourself in the kitchen?

Fogg It is extremely difficult to gas yourself on an electric stove. (*With sudden anger*) Yes! We both know why you crept in here using that key. Because you still suspect there's—there's—something between Di-Di—your wife and me.

Reaper Your wife? Very formal, aren't we, Mister Fogg?

Fogg All right. Diane. It's true I did—do—find Diane extremely—how shall I put it—um—very well, I'll say it—sexually attractive.

Reaper Oooo! Language!

Fogg But if you were honest with yourself you'd realize Diane merely needed a reliable shoulder to cry on and imagined she was in—fond of me on the rebound after finding out about your extra-ma—extra-mar—extraordinary behaviour with that girl in Amsterdam. (*He picks up the beans and pies and goes into the kitchen*)

Reaper follows him in. During the ensuing scene Fogg puts the pies down on the working surface, and puts the baked beans into a saucepan after filling it with water. (This is a trick saucepan and is described on page 65.) He places the saucepan on the stove and switches on the appropriate electric ring. Later he puts one pie in the refrigerator and the other into the oven, which he also switches on

Reaper There's nothing extraordinary about a bit on the side when it's offered you on a platter, which is why I say that if a girl as attractive as my Diane throws herself at you, you'd have to do it once—if only to be polite.

Fogg For the last time, I have never looked at another man's life in all my wife.

Reaper (*angrily*) What gets me is I'm prepared to forgive and forget, and you won't even admit it.

Fogg I certainly won't admit to something I didn't do, just to salve your conscience. (*He pushes past Reaper*) Now, if you'll excuse me I have to put something in the oven.

Reaper That'll be the day! All right, I accept your word.

Fogg leaves the kitchen and enters the bedroom. Reaper follows

Fogg (*slightly mollified*) Thank you.

Reaper But if I had definite proof Diane had been up to anything I'd kill her and the man. So watch your step, son.

Fogg If it satisfies you I had told Diane it is better we shouldn't meet for the time being.

Reaper Much better. By the way, are you going out tonight?

During the following Fogg undresses down to his shirt, underpants and socks, hanging his clothes up neatly in the wardrobe

Fogg No. I thought I'd take these clothes off and relax.

Reaper I should think so, you look like a refugee from Moss Bros' window. May I borrow that old car of yours?

Fogg My car again. Whatever for?

Reaper I'm going down to Paddington to visit my poor old aunt.

Fogg You seem to be getting very fond of your poor old aunt these days.

Reaper I've always been fond of her. Any objections?

Fogg No; but that's the second time this week.

Reaper It could be three times next week, if my health will stand it.

Fogg *Your* health?

Reaper Auntie's health. She gets very excited.

Fogg Why don't you use your own car?

Reaper Because I don't like leaving a Rolls outside a Paddington hotel— old folks' hot . . . hostel.

Fogg Why not?

Reaper Too flashy. (*Irritably*) Look, have you some objection to my borrowing that old banger? Damn it all, *I* sold it to you for peanuts.

Fogg N—no, but . . .

Reaper Then what are we arguing about? Let's have the keys. I'll pop them through the letter-box later.

Fogg produces the car keys and hands them over

Fogg How long will you be?

Reaper About eight hours.

Fogg Eight hours! You're keeping that old lady up till three in the morning?

Reaper Yes! She's an insomniac; can't sleep. Is the car still parked in Smedley's yard?

Fogg Yes.

They move back into the sitting-room

Reaper I'll go down through the shop. I need some cash from the small money safe.

Fogg I don't know how much there is.

Reaper Yesterday there was one thousand three hundred and four pounds seventeen pence and one Spanish peseta.

Fogg Remember, when you lock the shop door turn that second lock *twice* or you won't set the alarm correctly.

Reaper (*goosing him*) Have a good time with Sweetie.

Fogg There's no Sweetie . . . (*He does not bother to go on as Reaper exits*)

Reaper exits through the shop door

The front door buzzer sounds in the sitting-room. Fogg presses the button

Fogg Fogg.

Over the intercom comes Diane Reaper's voice, faintly distorted by the inter-com

Diane's Voice Oh, Foggy, it's Diane Reaper.

Fogg (*reacting*) Diane! Oh, hullo! You've just missed your husband.

Diane's Voice (*dismayed*) He's not there!

Fogg No, but you might catch him if you go round to the front. He's gone out through the shop.

Diane's Voice No! I don't want to see him. Come down and let me in. I'm in trouble.

Fogg I don't need to come down. It's automatic. (*He presses the button*) Just push. All right?

Fogg dashes into the bedroom, finds a dressing-gown, and hastens back to the sitting-room, putting it on as he goes

Diane enters through the front door. She is a luscious young blonde, with a splendid figure and a fair absence of brain

Diane, you really shouldn't have come here.

Diane Foggy, you must help me. I just had to see you.

She is in a shocking state. For a start she is soaked to the skin. Her short skirt is dirty, her top is torn. The knees of her stockings have holes in them. She has no top-coat. She carries a small handbag and a rolled-up glossy magazine

Fogg (*shocked*) Oh! Whatever happened to you?

Diane What didn't? For a start I got pushed out of a car into the gutter. (*She goes and sits on the sofa*)

Fogg Who did this?

Diane A nice kind gentleman. Mind you, I shouldn't have tried to scratch his eyes out—not while he was driving.

Fogg But you should go home and change.

Diane Go home? Like this? And risk Eddie finding out?

Fogg Finding out what? (*He sits beside her*)

Diane unrolls the magazine and hands it to him. A voluptuous nude is seen on the cover. Fogg reacts with disgust

But what are you doing with this awful rag? It's been banned.

Diane And the circulation's doubled since it was. Look.

Fogg But all these ladies are st-st-st . . . naked. Why are you showing me this?

Diane Before I married Eddie I used to be a model. Look at page nineteen.

Fogg starts to turn the pages, reacting in varying degrees of disgust at what he sees. He reaches the page and almost jumps out of his skin. He closes the magazine with a snap, looks at Diane, and away again

Fogg B-b-b-but that's . . .

Diane Yes. Me. I was bigger then.

Fogg Yes, I can see that. But when was this taken?

Diane Three years ago, but they're reissuing them, every week.

Fogg *Them*?

Diane They've got lots more pictures like it. Better than that.

Fogg Worse, you mean.

Diane Yes.

Fogg Did Eddie ever know . . . ?

Diane No. God forbid.

Fogg Oh dear! Well, perhaps if you made a clean breas . . . um, clean— um . . .

Diane Never! You know what Eddie is. Insanely jealous.

Fogg (*rising*) Yes, I do, and I don't feel at all happy about you being here.

Diane Don't worry, Foggy, I shan't fling myself at you again.

Fogg It's not that. I know you were just overwrought. It's Eddie. He still suspects the worst and I think he'd kill us if he found you here. What possessed a nice girl like you to be photographed like this?

Diane The difference between earning thirty-five quid a week and a hundred and fifty.

Fogg Is there no way of persuading the editor to stop publishing them?

Diane Yes. I can buy the negatives back.

Fogg How much?

Diane A thousand pounds by midday tomorrow—or else.

Fogg Or else what?

Diane Eddie gets copies of the lot.

Fogg Have you got a thousand?

Diane No, that's why I came to you, Foggy. You were the only person who might help me.

Fogg I haven't got a thousand on me. (*He throws the magazine on the floor above the armchair*)

Diane You could get it from the money safe below.

Fogg It's not my money. It's the *company's* money. Besides, Eddie knows to a Spanish peseta how much is in that safe, and he'll be going to the bank the day after tomorrow.

Diane Couldn't you replace it by then? Please, Foggy! I swear I'll pay you back somehow.

Fogg Well—all right. But . . .

Diane Oh, thanks. It's wonderful the way I can always turn to you.

She hugs him. He turns to jelly

Fogg M'yes. I just hope it doesn't turn out the way it did last time.
Diane Do you mind if I clean up here?
Fogg You'd better. You can't walk about looking like that. I'll go and get the money.

Fogg exits through the shop door

Diane immediately starts to strip off in the sitting-room. She removes her skirt and top, leaving herself in bra and panties. She removes her damaged stockings, examines them, and throws them into the wastepaper-basket. One of them hangs over the edge and is visible. She then walks into the kitchen and hangs the clothes on the hanger above the stove. She turns on the three remaining rings to give heat—one being already alight cooking the baked beans. This done she leaves the kitchen, walks across the sitting-room, picks up her shoes, opens the bedroom door and goes into the bedroom

Fogg enters through the shop door with a wad of money

Fogg Where are you?
Diane (*calling*) Just going to have a quick bath.
Fogg Righto.

Diane exits to the bathroom, closing the door

Fogg pockets the money and enters the kitchen. He looks at the drying clothes, smiles ruefully and shakes his head. He opens the oven to see how his pie is progressing

The front door opens and Reaper enters. He carries a bottle of champagne, which he puts down

Reaper (*loudly*) Fogg!

Fogg utters a muted yelp, freezes momentarily, then in a panic seizes Diane's clothes off the hanger, hurls them into the oven and slams the oven door. The noise of the oven door brings Reaper into the kitchen. Fogg turns guiltily to face him

Ah! There you are!
Fogg (*unnecessarily loudly*) Yes! (*Trying to act at ease, he puts his arms out to either side, and badly burns his left hand on one of the electric rings. He yells*)
Reaper I didn't know you could sing in Japanese. And why use four rings to heat one tin of baked beans?
Fogg Um—er. Testing. Just been converted to North Sea electricity. (*He pushes Reaper into the sitting-room*) That wasn't eight hours.
Reaper No. A funny thing happened . . .
Fogg Just a second. Something to do—put away—bedroom . . . Shan't be a moment. (*He rushes into the bedroom, slamming the door, and runs across to the bathroom door*)

Reaper removes his hat and coat and hangs them up

(*In a hoarse whisper*) Danger. Don't splash. He's back.

Diane (*off*) What?

Fogg (*in a hoarse whisper*) Sssh! Eddie. He's back. Don't splash . . .

Reaper enters the bedroom. Fogg straightens up, jumps away from the door and starts to sing

Splish, splash, splosh,
Mother's in the wash . . .
(*Speaking very loudly*) SO YOU'RE BACK, *EDDIE*. I DIDN'T
EXPECT YOU BACK YET, *EDDIE*. THIS IS A SURPRISE, *EDDIE*.

Reaper What are you shouting for?

Fogg hurries across and pushes Reaper back through the bedroom door into the sitting-room, closing the bedroom door behind him

Fogg Have a glass of bath water—have a drink?

Reaper Have *you* been drinking?

Fogg No. You know me. Never touch it.

Reaper Hmmm. Perhaps you'd act a bit more normal if you did.

Fogg Why have you come back?

Reaper To give you some very good news.

Fogg Oh? Yes, yes, yes.

Reaper You know that old car of yours?

Fogg Yes, yes, yes.

Reaper It's been stolen.

Fogg Oh, good, good, good. What! When? How?

Reaper (*showing the champagne bottle*) I parked it near the off-licence and
got out to buy a bottle of champagne. Just as I was leaving the shop,
two guys ran up, hopped into the car and drove off.

Fogg Didn't you lock it?

Reaper Lock *that* old heap? I must say you don't seem very grateful.

Fogg Why should I be grateful?

Reaper Look at the condition it was in. The bodywork was rattling, the
big ends were going. It can't be worth more than fifty quid and I'll
bet it's insured for about four hundred.

Fogg (*nodding, then reacting*) Then why did you sell it to me for five
hundred?

Reaper Don't change the subject. Better report it to the police.

Fogg Haven't you done that?

Reaper No. Of course not. I didn't want to risk them finding it. I was
thinking of you.

Fogg Oh, very kind I'm sure. (*He gives Reaper a look, then goes to the
telephone and dials, waiting as it rings*)

Reaper By the way, to make things easier, tell them it was you who was
driving.

Fogg Why?

Reaper Does it matter?

Fogg It doesn't matter—but why?

Reaper Why? Why? Why? All these questions!

Fogg Only one. Why? (*On the phone*) Hello. . . . Yes, police, please. (*To Reaper*) Well, why?

Reaper For a start, are you insured for any driver or just yourself?

Fogg I don't remember. I think . . .

Reaper There you are, then! Saved you a fortune in fines for driving an uninsured vehicle.

Fogg It *wasn't* uninsured and *I* wasn't driving it.

Reaper That makes it worse! *Encouraging* a third party to drive a vehicle knowing it to be uninsured.

Fogg (*shouting*) But I didn't encourage you!

Reaper The police don't know that, do they? You've had a narrow shave, son.

Fogg (*yelling*) But *I* know . . . (*On the phone*) Yes, hullo? . . . I wish to report the theft of a car. . . . Yes, mine. . . . A blue Ford Zephyr nineteen sixty-four. . . . The registration number? Um . . .

Reaper C-L-R one-seven-two B.

Fogg (*on the phone*) C-L-R one-seven-two B. It was parked near the off-licence in Hadrian's Road, S.W. three. . . . No, it wasn't locked. It was only left for a few minutes. . . . Who was driving? . . . Well, there were two of them, two men. . . . Oh, before—um—me, Fogg. . . . No, I am not talking about the weather. That happens to be my name. Roger Fogg. . . . Three Park Walk Mews, S.W. three. . . . Oh—um—just now. A few minutes ago. . . . Thank you very much. (*He hangs up, looking miserable*)

Reaper (*clapping him on the back*) Well done! That's put you in the clear.

Fogg Oh yes! Making me lie to the police.

Reaper I must say I'm hurt. I stick my neck out to save you losing your licence and that's all the thanks I get.

Fogg I'm sure you meant well. (*He pushes him towards the front door*) Now you'll be wanting to get along.

Reaper There's no rush.

Fogg Don't you want to see your aunt?

Reaper I've scrubbed that.

Fogg Oh. Well, I was just going to bed.

Reaper At a quarter past seven?

Fogg gives an exaggerated yawn

Fogg I'm very tired.

Reaper And what about your supper?

Fogg I like it in bed.

Reaper So do I, but what about your supper? You know, the pies and the baked beans? The orgy? I say, could I have a drink? All this lying on your behalf has made me thirsty.

Fogg If you insist. What would you like?

Reaper I'll have a large whisky.

Fogg I said "*what*" would you like. *I* will decide the quantity. (*He goes to pour a drink*)

Reaper's eyes fall on the wastepaper-basket, with Diane's stockings hanging out of it

Reaper Hullo, hullo, hullo! What's this?

Fogg sees them, too, and dashes forward

Fogg NOTHING!!

Reaper beats him to it, shoves him aside, and picks up the stockings

Reaper So that's why you wanted me out! You've got a bird here!
Fogg No!
Reaper Why didn't you tell me? I'd have pushed off right away.
Fogg There is no-one.
Reaper Must be a scrubber . . .!
Fogg No . . .
Reaper Yes! Holes in her stockings and you're only giving her baked beans . . .
Fogg There's no her. There's nobody.
Reaper Foggy, these are women's stockings. Now they weren't there before, because I dropped my cigar butt in there. Look! Now, they're not yours, are they?
Fogg Yes!
Reaper Pardon?
Fogg They are mine.
Reaper You wear women's stockings?
Fogg Not all the time.
Reaper But some of the time?
Fogg Yes.
Reaper Why?
Fogg I'm a trans-vest . . .
Reaper Tight!
Fogg Quite!
Reaper You mean to say you get your kicks out of dressing up as a woman?
Fogg Yes.
Reaper I knew there was something queer about you!
Fogg No! Not queer!
Reaper If dressing up as a woman isn't queer, I don't know what is. How did it start?
Fogg I prefer not to discuss it.
Reaper Oh come on! I've always been interested in odd balls.
Fogg If you must know, it was my mother: she wanted a daughter and used to call me—er—Sybil.
Reaper Sybil?
Fogg Yes.
Reaper It suits you.
Fogg Thank you.
Reaper (*laughing*) Well, this puts you in the clear about Diane at last. Fancy that!
Fogg You won't tell anyone, will you?
Reaper (*putting his hand on his heart*) Trust me.
Fogg The better type of client wouldn't like it.

Reaper Wouldn't wear it, either.

Fogg Do you mind leaving now?

Reaper Beginning to feel the itch? Coming on, is it, eh? (*He does a "swishy" movement with his hips*)

Fogg No! Good-bye.

Reaper Okay! Okay! (*He moves towards the front door*)

Fogg If the police get on to me, is there anything else I should tell them? I mean, did you leave anything in the car?

Reaper Um—I'm glad you mentioned that. There was one little thing.

Fogg Something valuable?

Reaper Well, expensive more than valuable. A bird.

Fogg What kind of bird?

Reaper The kind you wouldn't fancy. A girl.

Fogg Wha-at!

Reaper Yes. She lives near here so she was lying down in the back so as not to be seen. The crooks took her when they drove off. Obviously they didn't realize she was there.

Fogg B-B-But why didn't you tell me this?

Reaper I just did.

Fogg *Before!*

Reaper Didn't seem important . . .

Fogg Not important? You made me tell the police *I* was driving the car! Suppose something has happened to that girl?

Reaper You should have thought of that before you started lying like a trooper.

Fogg (*wildly*) I didn't know there was a girl in the car.

Reaper And I didn't know it was going to be stolen—so we're equally to blame.

Fogg But what am I going to tell the police?

Reaper Oh, don't mention it unless they bring it up!

Fogg You have landed me right in the——

Reaper (*interrupting*) Ah! Ah! Temper, Sybil, temper!

Fogg Yes, I am in a temper and I'm disgusted with you.

Reaper With me? Why? You have nothing to lose and I have. I'm married.

Fogg Yes! You, the jealous, suspicious husband, and look what *you* get up to? You're still at your little games.

Reaper Yes, you don't know what it's all about. You don't know what you're missing. Night-night, Sybil.

Reaper collects his hat and coat then exits through the front door

The moment the door has closed Fogg dashes into the bedroom and to the bathroom door

Fogg You can come out now.

The bathroom door opens and Diane comes out wrapped in a rather small bath towel. Fogg takes the money from his pocket. They stand above the bed

Diane Has he gone?

Fogg Yes, thank goodness! You must get dressed and go home. Here's the money to pay for your blackmail.

Diane Poor you! What a thing to happen.

Fogg Yes, dreadful. I honestly think he'd murder me if he saw you like this.

The front door opens immediately and Reaper enters

Reaper I'm back again, Foggy. It's only me.

Fogg gasps, pushes Diane into the bed, hurls himself on top of her and pulls up the eiderdown. He shoves the money under the pillow. Reaper walks to the bedroom door and looks through. (It is simpler to use a specially designed bed with a recess which Diane can slip into, thus heightening the impression that Fogg really lies on top of her.) Fogg, eiderdown up to his chin, stares at Reaper, wordless

You're up to something!

Fogg No.

Reaper (*advancing into the room*) Yes! You're blushing! What are you hiding under there?

Fogg Nothing. Go away.

Reaper You're up to something. I know! You've got them on again, haven't you? (*He makes the "swishing" movement*) Sybil's taken over. Let's have a look.

Fogg (*loudly*) If you touch me or my bed, I'll—I'll . . .

Reaper What? Scream?

Fogg No. Call the police and tell them who *really* drove my car.

Reaper I believe you would, you bitch! (*He grins*) I'm only kidding. (*Without knowing he does so, he picks up the rolling-pin where Ruff has left it*) I don't care what you get up to in your own . . . I'm enormously . . . (*He suddenly realizes he is holding the rolling-pin and draws some dreadful sexual connotation from its presence in Fogg's bedroom. He looks sick, drops it like a hot brick and surreptitiously wipes his hands on his raincoat as he speaks*) Yes. Well. I'll leave you to get on with—whatever it is. Ugh!

Reaper is about to move away when Diane evidently makes a violent movement and her two little feet pop out at the end of the bed. Reaper looks at them and does a double-take

I've never seen such tiny feet. Amazing! Like a woman's. (*He tickles the feet*)

Fogg desperately giggles. The feet suddenly withdraw beneath the eiderdown

All these years together, and I never knew you painted your toenails.

Reaper goes out of the bedroom and exits through the front door

Fogg waits for a moment then lifts the eiderdown a little and gets out of bed. He runs to the door, looks out, looks back. He has Diane's towel in his belt, but does not realize it. The inference is that she is now naked. (This is actually a towel of similar colour pre-set in the bed)

Fogg He's gone. You can come out now. (*No answer or movement from the bed*) Diane! (*He raises the eiderdown, looks horrified, and drops it. He tears the towel from his belt and thrusts it under the eiderdown*) Oh! Sorry—coming in on the blind side. (*Pause*) May I come in?

The eiderdown begins to move about, and finally Diane appears with the towel round her again. She is breathing rather hard and looks a bit groggy

Are you all right?

Diane (*nodding*) Yes. A minute more and I wouldn't have been. (*Dizzily*) Now where did I put my clothes?

Fogg They're in the . . . OH MY HAT! Wait there. (*He dashes out of the bedroom, across the sitting-room and into the kitchen*)

Diane What's up?

Fogg opens the oven door and a cloud of blinding smoke comes out. Coughing and spluttering, Fogg reaches in and hauls out the smoking, but still recognizable, ruins of Diane's clothes

The front door opens and Reaper enters and hangs up his coat and umbrella

Reaper Foggy. It's little ol' me again.

Fogg yelps

Diane leaps back into the bathroom, closing the door

Fogg picks up a large tureen and thrusts the smoking clothes into it. He starts to stir them with a wooden spoon. Reaper sniffs and goes into the kitchen. He stops, waving a hand across his face

What have you got there?

Fogg (*choking*) My supper.

Reaper A trifle overdone, wouldn't you say? (*He moves round to have a closer inspection*)

Fogg desperately turns his back to prevent Reaper seeing, moving to frustrate Reaper's inquisitive gaze. He adds salt and pepper, and to increase the impression that he is cooking he "tastes" from the spoon, shudders and chokes

What *are* you cooking?

Fogg I thought you'd gone. What do you want?

Reaper Got your smoke signal so came back.

Fogg Very funny. (*He makes another quick move to prevent Reaper getting a closer look*)

Reaper Actually forgot the champagne again. Why so shy? What *are* you cooking?

Fogg I'm trying to smoke something.

Reaper You succeeded. You'll have the fire brigade here in a minute.

Fogg Open the window, then.

Reaper You open. I'll stir.

Reaper gives Fogg a sudden shove, sending him off balance, seizes the spoon, delves into the tureen and fishes out Diane's blackened suspender-belt

Reaper Sybil?

Fogg That is smoked squid.

Reaper pulls it apart to make absolutely sure he is not imagining things, then places it against Fogg's midriff

Reaper No, Sybil. More like singed suspender-belt, the very latest in way-out dishes.

Fogg seizes the belt and throws it into the tureen

Fogg Oh, go away.

Reaper No! Let's have a party. There's plenty for all.

Fogg If you don't go now, I swear I'll turn nasty.

Reaper *Turn* nasty? Cooking girls' clothes! You can't get any nastier than that. Honestly, old cock, you should see a head-shrinker and get it shrunk.

Fogg I wasn't cooking them.

Reaper What were you doing, then?

Fogg Burning them.

Reaper Why?

Fogg (*throwing the clothes into the bin under the sink*) It was you, finding me out. It made me feel ashamed so I decided to burn them and turn over a new leaf.

Reaper There must be an easier way to get rid of them.

Fogg It was a symbolic act.

Reaper Sounds a lot of symbolics to me, but if that's your story you stick to it.

Fogg switches off the four electric rings

Fogg I will. (*Indicating the door*) Good night. (*He pushes Reaper back into the sitting-room*)

The front door buzzer sounds. Fogg answers it

    Fogg.

Ruff's voice comes, distorted, over the intercom

Ruff's Voice Mr Fogg? It's the police. About your car.

Fogg Oh! You'd better come up, officer. (*He presses the button*)

Reaper Blast! I hoped to be gone before they arrived. Now, keep your head.

Fogg It would be much better to tell the truth.

Reaper And admit to lying the first time? You're out of your mind.

There is a knock on the front door

Fogg Come in.

Ruff enters. Fogg's face expresses acute dismay

Oh! It's you.
Ruff (*pleasantly*) Yes. Evening again, sir.
Fogg (*glumly*) Yes. (*To Reaper*) The Inspector was here earlier about a tip-off on a possible burglary.

Ruff sniffs and grimaces

Ruff Is something burning?
Reaper Good evening. Don't worry about the smell. Fanny Cradock here had an accident. I'm Eddie Reaper, his partner.
Ruff (*taking Reaper's hand*) Inspector Ruff.
Reaper Arrived just ahead of you to hear the silly fellow had his car nicked.
Ruff Yes. (*To Fogg*) Since I was in the neighbourhood they sent me round to collect a few details.
Reaper That's service for you. Have they found the car yet?
Ruff Not yet, sir. (*To Fogg*) Forgive me, but I thought I understood you to say you weren't going out tonight?
Fogg Yes.
Ruff But you did?
Fogg Yes.

Reaper moves away so that he stands behind Ruff, who faces Fogg

Ruff Changed your mind?
Fogg Yes.
Ruff Could I ask where you were going, sir?
Fogg Yes.
Ruff (*patiently*) Where were you going?
Fogg To the off-licence.
Ruff Why?

Reaper signals to the champagne bottle

Fogg To buy a bottle of champagne.
Reaper (*pointing*) And there it is.
Ruff I thought you said you didn't drink, Mr Fogg?
Fogg I don't.
Ruff At the time, you were taking it on to someone else?
Fogg Um—no.
Ruff Where were you taking it, then?

Reaper indicates "here"

Fogg Here.
Ruff But you didn't intend to drink it?
Fogg No.

Reaper's expression betrays his obvious feeling that Fogg is doing very badly

Ruff Let me get this straight. You got your car out to drive down to the off-licence to buy a bottle of champagne to bring back here and *not* drink it. Right?
Fogg Right.

There is a long pause

Ruff ((*at last*) I see. Anyway, I don't know why I'm worrying about that. It's a free country, isn't it? If he wants to buy a bottle of champagne and not drink it, that's no concern of mine. (*He laughs*)

Reaper laughs, and Fogg tries to

Oh! Just one question! You do mean the off-licence a hundred yards down the road?

Reaper nods behind Ruff's back

Fogg Yes.
Ruff Wouldn't it have been easier to walk?
Fogg Why?
Ruff By the time you fetched the car, got into the car, out of the car, into it again, out again, parked it again . . .

While Ruff is talking Reaper, behind him, walks up and down with a pronounced limp

Fogg Limp. Limp!

Feeling he is dealing with a lunatic, Ruff walks and limps

No! No! Not you limp! Me limp!
Ruff Oh, you felt limp?
Fogg Yes, me felt limp.

Reaper angrily gestures "no"

No! Me—er . . .

Fogg looks at Reaper, who drags his leg grotesquely

Me want to go wee-wee.

Reaper furiously indicates "no!"

No! Me no want to go wee-wee. Apparently I've been.

Reaper again limps

I've got it! I've got a gammy leg!
Ruff Ah! I see, I see. A bad leg. I knew it must be something like that! I mean going to all that trouble to get the car out to drive a hundred yards doesn't make sense, does it?

Ruff laughs. Reaper laughs. Fogg again tries to, and sits

Wait a minute!

Fogg rises

Where do you garage your car?

Fogg In a builder's yard up the road. I have an arrangement with them.

Ruff You took it from there tonight?

Fogg Yes.

Ruff That would be Smedley's Yard?

Fogg Yes.

Ruff About five hundred yards up the road?

Fogg Yes.

Ruff Five hundred yards *in the opposite direction* to the off-licence?

Fogg opens his mouth to say "yes", then realizes he has fallen into a trap

Fogg (*uneasily*) In a way.

Ruff No, sir. You can only go *one way* in an opposite direction.

Fogg Yes—er—yes.

Ruff I must be awfully dense, Mr Fogg, but it seems to me that by using your car, you were giving yourself an extra thousand yards to walk on that gammy leg of yours: assuming you intended returning the car to the yard, of course.

Fogg is silent. Reaper snaps his fingers, nods his head admiringly, and takes out a pocket calculator

Reaper Inspector, I think you're right. Let's double-check. From here to yard five hundred; return from yard five hundred; walk from here to off-licence one hundred; return one hundred. Grand total of . . . (*He does a lot of tapping on the calculator*)

Ruff Twelve hundred yards.

Reaper toils on

Reaper (*much later*) Twelve hundred yards.

Ruff Take away the two hundred he'd have walked, if he hadn't used the car . . .

Reaper And the answer is . . .

Ruff One thousand yards.

Reaper (*after another long pause*) One thousand yards.

Ruff We can't afford those in the force.

Reaper No, they're very quick.

Ruff (*to Fogg*) Any comments, Mr Fogg?

Fogg You're wrong, actually. I only did *four* hundred extra yards.

Ruff How do you work that out?

Fogg If I hadn't used the car I'd have walked two hundred yards there and back. As it was, I walked five hundred yards to the yard, drove to the shop, then walked one hundred yards back. That's a total of six hundred yards.

Ruff He's right!

Reaper Take away the two hundred he'd have walked if he hadn't used the car—and the answer is—four million three hundred thousand and . . . My decimal point slipped, only *four* hundred unnecessary yards—and who's counting?

Ruff and Reaper both laugh genially. Fogg sits again, and again tries to join in, hoping the worst has passed. Ruff's laugh stops abruptly

Ruff Wait a minute!

Fogg rises

He only walked four hundred unnecessary yards because his car was stolen. If it hadn't been stolen he'd have walked *my* thousand unnecessary yards.

Fogg Ah, but I didn't!

Ruff True! True! Do I take it, then, that you *knew* your car was going to be stolen?

Fogg Yes—NO!

Ruff No. Therefore, Mr Fogg, you did set out with the intention of walking a thousand unnecessary yards. We're right back to where we started.

Reaper I think you should tell the Inspector the truth, Foggy.

Fogg (*eagerly*) About time! You see, it wasn't m——

Reaper (*cutting in swiftly*) The truth is, his doctor said to him: "Foggy," he said, "you *must* exercise that leg by walking at least . . ."

Ruff A thousand yards a day?

Reaper Precisely.

Ruff Then why bother to use the car at all?

Reaper Because he's bloody lazy.

Ruff gives them a look

Ruff Mr Fogg, were you sorry to hear that your car had been stolen?

Fogg Not really.

Ruff May I see your registration book, sir?

Fogg Eh?

Ruff The car log-book.

Fogg Ah, that. Sit down, Inspector. (*He limps away, but on the wrong leg*)

Ruff Wrong leg, sir!

Fogg limps back, and then limps forward again on the right leg

Fogg I'm not much of a car man. In fact, I hardly ever used it. It's pretty old, rather rusty and the tyres are worn to shreds.

Ruff Really? Smooth, eh?

Fogg (*nodding*) Not an inch of tread on them. Until I made up my mind whether I was going to keep the car or not there was no point in buying new tyres.

Ruff Except to save yourself a hefty fine. Defective tyres constitute a serious offence, you know.

Fogg Oh!

Ruff However, that won't arise unless we find the car.

Fogg nods, rummages in a drawer, finds the log-book and limps back to hand it over

That's the right one, sir. Well done.

Fogg There you are, that's the motor vehicle thing, and the insurance thing . . .

Ruff opens out a white paper which is inside the log-book and frowns. Meanwhile, Fogg limps—on both legs—to sit on the sofa

Ruff This is a temporary cover note for fourteen days only.

Fogg Yes, I told you, I hadn't made up my mind whether I was going to keep the car or not.

Ruff But this is two and a half months out of date, sir. Did you renew it?

Fogg Oh! No, I don't think . . .

Reaper Foggy! Foggy!

Fogg An oversight. I use the car so seldom, as I told you . . .

Ruff Sorry, sir. You've admitted to driving while uninsured. (*He searches the log-book*) Where's your MOT?

Fogg My what?

Ruff MOT. Certificate of road-worthiness. Like that. (*He produces one*)

Fogg Oh, that pretty thing.

Ruff Yes, that pretty thing, except this one's pretty well out of date.

Fogg Oh my goodness—I clean . . . Oh dear . . .

Ruff (*wearily*) I suppose the car was licensed?

Fogg Oh, yes . . . (*He realizes it wasn't*) I don't know.

Ruff gives him a look, and makes noises

Ruff Oh dear, not licensed, no MOT, uninsured and smooth tyres.

Fogg I was going to get the brakes seen to.

Ruff (*copying*) C-L-R one-seven-two B. Mm. That's interesting. (*He hands the log-book back*) Thank you, sir.

Fogg (*floundering*) With all these things—shall I . . .? Will I . . .?

Ruff Let's put it this way, sir. I wouldn't contemplate buying a new car for at least twelve months. (*Suddenly*) Were you alone tonight?

Fogg (*guiltily*) When?

Ruff In the car?

Fogg Er—there was nobody with *me* in the car tonight.

Ruff I see, I see. Thank you, much obliged. C-L-R one-seven-two B.

Reaper and Fogg both look relieved. Ruff puts away his notebook and adopts a friendly, conversational air

Oh, by the way, funny thing happened tonight. As I told you, sir, I planted one of my men on a roof near here—in case there was anything in this Quiet Gang tip-off. My constable saw a man and a girl approach a car in a yard. Imagine my constable's surprise when the girl gets into the back of the car and lies full length on the floor. The man gets in front and drives off. (*He chuckles*)

Reaper and Fogg are both very still

Well, no-one was breaking the law, so my constable simply contented himself with taking down the number of the car. (*To Fogg*) You'll never guess what the number was.

Reaper Let me try. C-L-R one-seven-two B!

Ruff Spot on, sir! C-L-R one-seven-two B. A nineteen sixty-four blue Zephyr. Well, Mr Fogg?

Ruff looks at Fogg. Fogg looks at Ruff, then at Reaper

Reaper Inspector, you have answered a lot of questions. (*To Fogg*) Foggy, admit it, you had a girl in the car, didn't you? You weren't alone. That's who this champagne was for and you weren't coming back. You were going on somewhere else with naughty, naughty thoughts in your mind.

Fogg (*furiously*) I have had it!

Reaper In the back of the car?

Fogg No! I've had enough! I won't go on with this.

Fogg turns towards Ruff, but Reaper breaks in fast, forcing a hearty laugh

Reaper I don't see why! *You've* nothing to be ashamed of. *You* aren't married. (*With meaning*) Now, if it had been *me* I'd have every reason to deny it. (*With another laugh, to Ruff*) Well, I must push off home. My wife's waiting for me. I'll just use your bathroom. (*He heads towards the bedroom door*)

Fogg gives a yelp and forestalls him

Fogg No, no. You can't use it, it's mine! It's mine! I have not left it in the condition in which I would like you to find it. All right, I admit it. I'll admit anything, but you've got to stay here and hear me admit it.

Ruff You admit you had a girl in the car?

Fogg Yes.

Ruff Thank you very much.

Reaper There you are, Inspector, mystery solved.

Ruff Not quite. What happened to her?

Fogg She—went off with the car.

Ruff Drove it off? Stole it?

Fogg No.

Ruff You don't mean she was driven off?

Fogg Yes.

Ruff Kidnapped, in fact?

Fogg Well—by mistake.

Ruff Why didn't you report this earlier?

Reaper Yes. Why didn't you report this earlier?

Fogg I forgot.

Ruff You forgot a girl had been kidnapped?

Fogg Yes.

Ruff Until this minute?

Fogg Yes. I had so much on my mind.

Ruff More important than a kidnapped girl who could be murdered? (*No answer*) What's her name?

Fogg looks blank. Behind Ruff, Reaper gets himself into a begging position then puts one hand to his seat. He mouths a silent bark

Fogg Her name is Neill . . .

Reaper violently wags his behind

No! Wagg! Tail! Neill Wagtail.

Ruff reacts, but writes. Reaper vehemently shakes his head, wags furiously, and again mouths a bark. Fogg desperately tries to follow him

A dog. Neill Wagtail's piano-playing dog.
Ruff Dog?
Fogg Dog.
Ruff Are you telling me she is a dog, or is called **Dog**, Mr Fogg?

Reaper again shakes his head. He continues silently to bare his teeth

Fogg No. Snarl.

Reaper shakes his head, indicates he's getting warm, and continues to lead him

Bay ... Growl ...
Ruff What are you playing at?
Fogg It's a game. You've got to guess.
Ruff This is no time for guessing games! Just tell me her name, sir.
Fogg Try it once. I'm sure you'll be good at it.

Reaper gets down on his knees, begs, wags a tail and barks silently. Fogg copies him exactly

Ruff What are you doing down there? (*He feels he is in a mad-house*)
Barker.

Fogg and Reaper leap to their feet and stick both thumbs in the air

Fogg Right first time. Barker!
Reaper Oh! Your friend, Mrs Barker, Foggy! Naughty boy! (*To Ruff*)
Married woman.

Ruff starts to write

Diane, wrapped in her towel, creeps from the bathroom, and tiptoes across the bedroom towards the connecting door, with the evident intention of peeking through the keyhole. She bends down, standing very near the burglar alarm bell which is on the wall behind her

Ruff Mrs Barker. Her age?
Reaper I must be going. It's *twenty* to *eight*. (*He signals to his watch*)
Ruff Her age, Mr Fogg?
Fogg Twenty to eight.
Ruff Huh?
Fogg Twenty-two.

Reaper shakes his head

Twenty-eight.
Ruff Blonde or brunette?
Fogg Definitely.

Ruff Which?
Fogg Brunette.

Reaper shakes his head

. . . In a blondish kind of way.

Ruff tears off a sheet of his notebook and throws it away

Ruff Which?
Fogg Blonde.

Reaper indicates "big boobs" with his hands

She's got arthritis. A big blonde with arthritis.

The burglar alarm sounds loudly. The bell in the bedroom sounds right beside Diane, scaring her badly. She emits a little scream

Ruff Break-in!

Ruff exits through the shop door

Fogg makes to follow Ruff, but Reaper pulls him back. The bell stops ringing as Fogg turns it off

Reaper Come here!
Fogg There's a break-in.
Reaper He'll take care of it. It's his job and it'll take his mind off our problems. (*He looks towards the bedroom*) What are you up to? Twenty-two, twenty-four, twenty-eight! Playing Bingo? Fogg, you've got a girl hidden here. You're stripped for action.
Fogg No I'm not! I've got my socks on!
Reaper Why are you hiding her from me? It's Diane, isn't it, and she's in the bathroom!

Fogg tries to stop Reaper, but Reaper pushes him aside and throws open the bedroom door, pushing Diane back against the wall and concealing her

Fogg (*desperately*) I don't know how she got there! I don't know how she got there! I didn't know she was there!

Fogg follows Reaper into the bedroom. Reaper, finding the bedroom apparently empty, suspects the bathroom and heads for that door

Reaper disappears into the bathroom

Diane grabs Fogg. Fogg gasps and drags her into the sitting-room, slamming the connecting door

Reaper emerges from the bathroom

Reaper starts a systematic search of every conceivable hiding-place in the bedroom. Fogg rushes Diane into the kitchen, opens the door of the broom cupboard, and thrusts Diane inside

Diane (*resisting*) No! I can't breathe in confined spaces.
Fogg Then hold your breath.

Fogg slams the cupboard door, rushes out of the kitchen and back into the bedroom where Reaper searches

Fogg No-one, you see?
Reaper I heard a female scream.
Fogg That was me.
Reaper Not unless you've recently tangled with a shark and lost. You've got a bird here, somewhere. I've a nose for these things. Why did you yell: "I don't know how she got there"?
Fogg Because I wouldn't.
Reaper Wouldn't what?
Fogg Wouldn't know how she got there if she had been there.

Fogg and Reaper go into the sitting-room

Reaper If *who* hadn't been there?
Fogg Whoever wasn't.
Reaper Whoever wasn't? That doesn't make sense.
Fogg Yes, it does. I wouldn't have known who was there even if there had been someone there. But there wasn't—was she? (*He moves to the shop door*) I say, I say, it's very quiet down there. I hope he's all right.
Reaper We'd have heard yells if he wasn't. It's this ruddy alarm. Always going off for no reason.
Fogg Just the same, I think I should go down and see . . .

Ruff enters through the shop door, stopping Fogg. He carries the cat

Ruff False alarm. Your cat was the culprit.
Fogg Oh, Sweetie!
Reaper Sweetie? You call your *cat* Sweetie?
Fogg (*taking the cat*) Yes, I'll put her in the kitchen. (*He goes into the kitchen, closing the door*)
Reaper Good work, Inspector. This calls for a drink.
Ruff (*drily*) That's a very good idea, sir.

Reaper helps himself to a drink of whisky and water. Ruff clears his throat in expectation. Fogg, in the kitchen, opens the closet door

Fogg (*in a whisper*) Diane. Won't be long now. Take this cat, will you.
Diane (*with a squeak*) No! I'm allergic to cats. Can't bear them near me. Take it away.

Fogg makes an angry exclamation, shuts the cupboard door, and turns back. He is tempted to put the cat in both the refrigerator and the oven, but refrains

Ruff Thirsty weather, sir.
Reaper Yes. (*Drinking*) Cheers.

Ruff stops as Fogg enters from the kitchen, still carrying the cat

Ruff I thought you were locking that cat in the kitchen.

Fogg I am—was—but I can't leave her there. She's allergic.

Reaper *Who's* allergic?

Fogg The cat. To kitchens. I'll put her in the bathroom. She's soaking wet. Oh, you naughty pussy. I hope it's only rain. Now I'll have to go and change.

Fogg goes through the bedroom and exits to the bathroom, where he leaves the cat. He then returns to the bedroom and during the following changes into trousers and a shirt

Ruff Mr Reaper, don't take this amiss. It's natural enough to back up a friend, but when someone's telling as many lies as Mr Fogg, it can be a risky occupation.

Reaper I appreciate that, Inspector. But that girl in his car was a married woman, and he probably doesn't want her husband to find out.

Ruff The husband will find out if she's found dead or injured.

Reaper sits down—on Ruff's hat

Reaper (*wanly*) Yes, but let's not think about that.

Ruff Well, we have to take these things into consideration. There's one or two little things I want to check up on. Excuse me, sir. You're sitting on my hat.

Reaper (*rising*) Lucky it wasn't your helmet.

Ruff (*rescuing his hat*) Well, I'll be on my way; but if you can persuade your friend to be a little more forthcoming I should be glad to hear from you.

Reaper Rely on me.

Ruff Good night, sir.

Ruff nods and exits through the front door

Reaper picks up the bottle of whisky and pours himself another measure. He finds there is no water in the jug—it has run out. He walks into the kitchen, carrying his glass. His back is turned to the stove. Fogg, now dressed, moves to the connecting door. Reaper sings, to give a sound cue for what follows

Reaper (*singing*) Oh, how we danced on the night we were wed,
                    We danced and we danced, 'cos the room had no bed . . .

Suddenly, with an explosion like a small bomb, the overheated tin of baked beans explodes. (Two "bombs" should be ready in case of one failing) Reaper cries out, falls to his knees, and splashes himself with water from the glass. Diane looks briefly out of the closet, terrified, sees Reaper, and disappears again. Fogg rushes into the kitchen, horrified

Fogg No! No! What happened? What happened, what happened?

Reaper Your bloody baked beans exploded.

Fogg Oh, thank God! I thought you'd shot her.

Reaper Shot who?

Fogg Di—Di—Dicky.

Reaper Dicky? Who the hell is Dicky?

Fogg My pussy.

Reaper You call your pussy "Dickie"? Of course, I suppose you would, Sybil. I thought you said her name was Sweetie?

Fogg I call her Dicky for short.

Reaper I thought you'd put her in the bathroom.

Fogg I did.

Reaper Then how could I shoot her in the kitchen?

Fogg You couldn't. I lost my head for a minute when I thought I heard a gun.

Reaper Silly question, I know, but why should you think I had a gun in the kitchen?

Fogg Yes. Why? Ridiculous. Forget it.

Reaper Forget it! I'm nearly killed with your secret weapon! Battered to bits with baked beans. Soaked to the skin, and you say, "Forget it", Earch! You, you—nit! (*He walks back into the sitting-room*)

Fogg hovers in the kitchen doorway, talking towards Diane in the cupboard

Fogg Stick it!

Reaper I heard that.

Fogg Then I take it back.

Reaper There's something up. I can smell it.

Fogg I'm just jittery. It's the cat going off and the beans and that alarm and everything. Good lord, I do believe I hear someone down below.

Reaper That's great. A two-thousand-pound alarm, and it doesn't even go off.

Reaper moves through the shop door

Fogg seizes on this with delight. He now speaks in a very loud voice for Diane's benefit

Fogg Yes! WE'LL BOTH GO AND LEAVE THE FLAT EMPTY NOW.

Reaper returns

Reaper I know we are. Come on!

Reaper exits

Fogg BORROW SOME OF MY CLOTHES TO GO HOME AS YOU CAN'T WEAR YOURS.

Reaper returns

Reaper Why can't I wear mine?

Fogg starts to shout, then returns to his normal voice

Fogg BECAUSE ... You said they were soaking.

Reaper They're not as soaking as that. Come on.

Reaper exits

Fogg (*yelling again*) RIGHT! WE'RE GOING DOWNSTAIRS TO-GETHER *NOW*!

Reaper returns

Reaper I know we are! Will you stop shouting! What's the matter with you?
Fogg I've got a sore throat.
Reaper Then why shout?
Fogg I want to make sure my voice is still there.

Fogg yells a last message as Reaper drags him off

WE SHAN'T BE LONG. TESTING. HAVE TO BE QUICK.

Fogg and Reaper exit

Diane emerges from the cupboard. She looks for her clothes but cannot see them. She peeks into the sitting-room, then runs across into the bedroom. She goes to the built-in cupboard and takes out a shirt. She carries this to the bathroom door and half enters. She sees something which causes her to shudder. She throws the shirt aside on the bed, then bends and picks up the cat from inside the bathroom. Holding it at arm's length she leaves the bedroom and heads back towards the kitchen

Diane Sorry, pussy, but I don't want a rash, too.

She enters the kitchen and puts the cat into the broom cupboard, closing the door. She runs back into the bedroom and goes through the connecting door, only half closing it, one second before Fogg and Reaper return

Fogg and Reaper enter through the shop door

Fogg Congratulations again! The door of the shop not even locked at all. It's a miracle we weren't burgled.
Reaper We weren't, so let's forget it.

Fogg hovers shiftily near the kitchen door

Fogg (*singing*) Have you gone away?
It's a rainy day—
Hip hip hip hooray!

No answer

Their voices have scared Diane, who dives back into the bathroom

Reaper What are you practising for? *The Sound of Music*. One of the nuns, no doubt. The stockings'll come in handy. I just don't know how you can sail through life! Me, I'm worried sick about Diane.

Fogg (*guiltily*) Won't Diane be safely at home watching the telly?

Reaper Not my *wife* Diane. The girl who was kidnapped in the car. She's my fiancée.

Fogg Your fiancée? You can't have a wife and a fiancée!

Reaper Well, you can't have two wives. Her name's Diane, too. Comes in very handy, at times. I talk in my sleep and I'm shocking about names.

Fogg You shock me altogether.

From the kitchen broom cupboard comes a definite crashing noise. Fogg and Reaper react to it. They start a race to the kitchen. Fogg wins, and places himself in a heroic position against the broom cupboard. Reaper follows him in

Reaper What have you got in there?

Fogg No, no, no!

Reaper Out of my way.

Fogg NOBODY here.

Reaper No, but there's somebody in there. Stand aside.

Fogg No, there isn't. It's only a broom cupboard.

There comes another crashing noise from inside the broom cupboard

Reaper What was that, David Broome on his horse?

Fogg No—pussy.

Reaper (*gently*) Pussy's in the bathroom, remember?

Fogg She—might have crept back.

Reaper Through three closed doors?

Fogg N-no . . .

Reaper Then how?

Fogg Mouse holes.

Reaper And mouse holes to you.

Reaper seizes Fogg. Fogg resists desperately

Fogg I swear I didn't remove her clothes. I did not remove her clothes. I did not remove *her* clothes.

Reaper hurls Fogg aside and opens the cupboard door. He looks inside. Fogg closes his eyes and awaits his doom. Reaper stares. Silence. Reaper bends into the cupboard and picks up the cat. Fogg is dumbfounded

Reaper How *did* she get back here?

Fogg opens his mouth

If you say mouse holes again I'll belt you.

Fogg She's very clever.

Reaper She's very *eerie*. That's impossible.

Fogg I'll put her out on the roof.

Reaper (*handing the cat over*) That's the only sensible thing you've said tonight.

Fogg She has a boy-friend out there.

Reaper I suppose they sit up there and he tells her about his operation?

Fogg (*opening the window*) I don't think he's had one. That's why she's fond of him. (*He puts the cat out of the window*) There we go.

Reaper What's the betting she breaks into the shop from the outside and sets the alarm off again?

Fogg No. She's like you, she'll have other things on her mind. (*Feeling happy and relieved*) Well, that's another mystery solved.

Reaper Mmmmm—mmmmmm. *One* mystery, but not all. (*He goes into the sitting-room*)

Fogg takes a last, relieved look into the cupboard, closes the door and follows Reaper into the sitting-room

Foggyboy. Who did you think was in that cupboard?

Fogg No-one.

Reaper We both heard sounds, didn't we?

Fogg Yes, pussy.

Reaper Does pussy wear clothes?

Fogg No.

Reaper Then why did you say, "I swear I did not remove her clothes"?

Fogg I wasn't talking about pussy then.

Reaper (*still gently*) Who *were* you talking about?

Fogg Nobody!

Reaper takes him by the scruff of the neck and pulls him close

Reaper I'm losing patience, Fogg. You said, "I swear I didn't remove her clothes."

Fogg (*struggling*) Yes. That's right. Those other clothes. The ones I cooked.

Reaper What about them?

Fogg I didn't remove them. They're still in the kitchen.

Reaper So what?

Fogg Nothing. I thought you'd like to know.

Reaper Why?

Fogg Well, you are my partner.

Reaper You're up to something.

Fogg All right. Search the flat. Go on.

Reaper I will.

Fogg Do!

Reaper looks at him closely. Fogg does not flinch. He is now confident that Diane has escaped

Reaper exits through the shop door. Diane emerges from the bathroom. She picks up Fogg's shirt from the bed prior to putting it on, and moves to the bathroom door

Fogg, feeling in command, sits in an easy chair and gestures airily as Reaper returns

Reaper enters from the shop door and opens the bedroom door

Go on, Eddie. Search the place. Try the bathroom.

Reaper The bathroom? Right. Double bluff, eh?

Diane, hearing this, darts away from the bathroom door and dives into the wardrobe

Reaper goes through the bedroom and exits to the bathroom

Fogg (*calling out happily*) Or the wardrobe!

Diane charges out of the wardrobe and dives under the bed

Reaper enters from the bathroom, heads to the wardrobe, and looks inside

Or what about under the bed?

Reaper turns from the wardrobe and kneels down. As he climbs under the bed Diane emerges from the other side and darts behind the window curtains. Reaper emerges from under the bed

Behind the curtains, perhaps?

Reaper heads towards the curtains and it seems that Diane is doomed, when he gives up

Reaper Ah, shut up! Let's try the only place you haven't mentioned. (*He comes from the bedroom, walks to the front door, seizes the handle, and wrenches the door open and looks out*)

Reaper exits through the front door. Diane comes out from behind the curtains and returns to the bathroom

Fogg suddenly notices the glossy dirty magazine. His new-found confidence evaporates in an instant. He jumps up, opens the magazine, tears out the offending page and, turning his back to the doors, throws the magazine into the wastepaper-basket

Reaper enters and kicks the door shut

Fogg crumples up the page and stuffs it in his mouth. He starts to chew manfully. Reaper does not notice this

Reaper You've managed to get rid of her. I don't know how you do it! You're up to something. You're lying again. You've got that stupid look on your face again.

Fogg keeps his back to Reaper, who advances on him again

Reaper What's this?

Fogg (*indistinctly*) Nothing.

Reaper pushes him aside, reaches down and picks up the magazine. He goggles at its contents

Reaper Well! Well! Sybil, you're a man of many parts. One of these girls you? (*He opens a page and reacts*) Phew! (*He turns the pages fast*)

I've never seen anything . . . (*He whistles, turns another page, reacts*)
There's a page missing. (*He looks up*) What happened to page nineteen?
I bet that's the best one. Come on! Where have you hidden it?

*Fogg has managed to swallow it. He opens his mouth to speak and lets out a
tremendous burp*

You've eaten it! You've eaten page nineteen. On both sides? Incredible!
(*He shakes his head*) I've just realized what a dull life I lead.

The front door buzzer sounds

Fogg Excuse me—that's me.
Reaper I'm not surprised—eating all that paper.

Fogg moves to the intercom and answers

Fogg Yes? Hic! Pardon?
A Woman's Voice (*on the intercom*) Foggy, it's Diane.

Fogg and Reaper both react. Reaper throws the magazine away.

Fogg Diane! I thought you'd . . . Why have you come b . . . here?
Woman's Voice Let me in, please. It's pouring.

Fogg hesitates, then presses the button

Fogg It's—er—your wife.
Reaper I know that, don't I? But what the devil's she doing here?
Fogg (*shakily*) I don't know. She's never been here before.
Reaper Yes, she has.
Fogg I swear she hasn't!
Reaper She has! With *me*—when I had this flat.

*Fogg approaches the front door nervously. It opens suddenly, pushing him
aside*

*Diane Barker—a sexy blonde—enters. Her clothes are in much the same
state as Diane Reaper's on her first entrance. In her hand she carries a
paper packet known in the jewellery world as a "stone parcel"; they are
used to carry diamonds. She wears a red and green striped shirt and blue
trousers. Her clothes are soaking. She either ignores the amazed Fogg or
does not see him. She runs straight to a dismayed-looking Reaper and
flings her arms around his neck*

Mrs Barker Oh, Foggy! Darling Foggy! I've had such a dreadful time
since I was kidnapped in your car. Foggy, Foggy, I thought I'd never
see you again. Oh, my Foggy.
Fogg F-F-Foggy? F-Fogg . . . *Foggy*!

*Fogg stiffens and his mouth opens. Mrs Barker dissolves into tears on
Reaper's chest. Reaper looks at Fogg over her shoulder and makes a half-
apologetic grimace, as—*

the CURTAIN *falls*

ACT II

The same. The action is continuous

Mrs Barker and Reaper are in the same embrace, with her head on his chest and him looking towards the outraged Fogg

Mrs Barker Oh, Foggy! I was never so scared in my life. They drove like maniacs, Foggy.

Fogg finds his voice at last, and it grows louder as he advances on them

Fogg Foggy? Foggy? FOGGY!!

Reaper releases Mrs Barker and moves quickly to Fogg, patting him on the head like a dog

Reaper Yes! Yes! Here I am. (*To Mrs Barker*) Very excitable. Di-Di, dear, this is my partner—Eddie Reaper.

Fogg REAPER!!! REAPER!!! REAPER!!!

Reaper Knows his own name, too! Isn't he clever? Eddie, this is my good friend Diane Barker.

Mrs Barker Good friend! We can tell him, can't we, Foggy? (*To Fogg*) We're going to be married as soon as I get my divorce.

Fogg You're mad!

Reaper Eddie! That's *rude*. (*To Mrs Barker*) Now, tell us what happened.

Mrs Barker Well, I was lying hidden in the car when these two men—burglars, they were—jumped in. They'd just done a job and their get-away car wouldn't start. They drove off without realizing I was hidden in the back.

Reaper Tck! What a world, eh, Eddie?

Mrs Barker After a while they saw a police car on their tail. They panicked and started to drive very fast; a tyre blew, and we crashed into an island and the car was wrecked.

Fogg Wrecked. Oh!

Mrs Barker They ran off with the police chasing them. I waited a minute, then got out and crept away.

Reaper (*worried*) Did you report it?

Mrs Barker How could I? It would have meant Jim finding out about us, and you know what he is.

Reaper Yes. (*To Fogg*) Her husband Jim's an all-in wrestler. Could have broken his heart.

Fogg (*nastily*) And your neck.

Mrs Barker approaches Fogg

Mrs Barker Don't think too badly of me, Eddie. You see, my husband's one of those freaks who play around but would murder me if he thought I was up to anything.

Fogg (*looking at Reaper*) I know the type. The worst.

Mrs Barker (*winningly*) Foggy says you're a wonderful friend. I'm sure I can trust you.

Fogg I'll do nothing to harm *you*.

Reaper Good old Foggy Oggy Eddie! (*To Mrs Barker*) How did you get back, Di-Di?

Mrs Barker Well, I walked. No money. I lost my bag somewhere—in the car, I expect.

Reaper Anything to identify you in it?

Mrs Barker No, only my nightie. (*She looks at Fogg*) We were going to a hotel.

Fogg I can't think why you bothered with the nightie.

Reaper That's what I said. It was a Trust House. (*His voice trails off as he notices the stone parcel in her hand*) Hey! Di-Di! What are you doing with that stone parcel?

Mrs Barker Stone . . .? Oh, this. Those crooks chucked it in the back as they got into the car. If it's their loot they didn't get away with much.

Reaper takes the parcel and quickly opens it. He looks inside and whistles

Reaper Not much! These are diamonds, love. Worth a fortune. (*He shows the parcel to Fogg*)

Mrs Barker How much?

Reaper Let's have a look. Nice stone—one carat twenty. Worth about three-and-a-half thousand pounds.

Mrs Barker And there must be forty of 'em and all.

Fogg That's over a hundred thousand pounds! You'll have to report it now.

Reaper I won't. She can post them anonymously to the police tomorrow.

Reaper hands back the parcel to Mrs Barker, who pockets it, unnoticed by Reaper and Fogg

Fogg No! I'll not keep stolen property in my flat.

Mrs Barker *Your* flat?

Fogg Yes, *my* flat and——

Reaper (*cutting in*) He's my landlord, darling. I rent it off him.

Fogg Augh! This is ridiculous!

Reaper Keep calm, old son. If there should be any trouble, naturally I'll see you're not involved.

Fogg Oh yes! I'm sure I can rely on you.

Reaper As always.

Mrs Barker Please, Mr Reaper. I know we must seem awful; but if we return the diamonds we're not doing anybody any harm, are we?

Fogg I warn you, that detective who was here is already suspicious.

Mrs Barker Detective?

Reaper Not to worry. He called about the car and he's gone. No reason to expect him back.

Mrs Barker Foggy . . .

Reaper } Yes? { (*Speaking together*)
Fogg

Reaper gives Fogg a look and Fogg angrily turns away, snapping his fingers

Mrs Barker I'd love to get my clothes off.

Reaper Yes.

Fogg No!

Mrs Barker And have a bath.

Fogg NO!

Reaper Eddie, what's got into you?

Fogg Haven't we had enough trouble—with clothes and drying—I mean look what happened last time . . .

Reaper With your dresses? (*He does his "swishing" movement*) We must just see it doesn't happen again, mustn't we, Sybil? I take it you have no valid objection to Mrs Barker using *my* bathroom?

Fogg flaps his arms helplessly

Diane emerges from the bathroom and peeks through the keyhole of the connecting door

Fogg No. No. Anyway, it's empty. She's gone now.

Reaper (*sharply*) Who's gone?

Fogg Um—pussy. Oh, hell!

Reaper Pussy? Forgive him, Di-Di. He's got pussies on the mind. Come this way.

Diane flees and hides behind the bedroom curtains. Reaper leads Mrs Barker to the bedroom door and shows her in

Bathroom's through there. Make yourself at home.

Mrs Barker Thanks. (*During the ensuing scene, she strips off*)

Reaper closes the door and hurries to Fogg

Reaper If I gave you fifty pence you wouldn't like to go to the pictures for half an hour, would you?

Fogg No! Now listen, don't you realize what this means? It was probably the Quiet Gang who took my car after their own broke down.

Reaper Probably.

Fogg This girl may be able to give descriptions which could lead to their arrest and conviction.

Reaper Sorry, chum. I'm not risking my wife Diane finding out about this one. Comes too soon after the trouble in Amsterdam.

Diane appears from behind the curtains and looks at Mrs Barker

Fogg And may I also ask why you are using my name for—for immoral purposes?

Reaper That's obvious, isn't it?

Fogg Not to me.

Reaper Di-Di lives locally. Someone's sure to mention the name of Eddie Reaper and the fact that he's married. Roger Fogg isn't.

Fogg You're unbelievable!

Reaper Damn it, man! I haven't stolen your name. I only borrowed it.

Fogg Like my car—and that's wrecked, too.

Reaper As to the car, I didn't want to park a ruddy great Rolls with the number R-E-A one P outside some crappy Paddington hotel.

Fogg What was it she said? "We're going to get married!" How are you going to get out of this one when you're tired of it?

Reaper Dunno. The sudden discovery of an incurable disease sometimes works a treat.

Fogg You are an absolute ba-ba . . .

Reaper Black sheep?

Fogg Amongst other things.

Reaper Yes, I know.

By this time Mrs Barker has stripped down. Carrying her clothes, she goes to the bedroom door and opens it. Diane peeps out of the curtains again

Mrs Barker Foggy, darling?

Automatically reacting to his name, Fogg goes to the door

Dry these, will you? Oh, hello. They're sopping, and I must go home in what I went out in. (*She thrusts her clothes into Fogg's arms, closes the door and goes to the bathroom*)

Mrs Barker exits into the bathroom

Fogg stands angrily with the clothes in his arms

Reaper Be a good chap and deal with them. Remember, they're not yours —so no more frying tonight.

Trembling with rage, Fogg walks forward and passes Reaper. Words fail him and he enters the kitchen, slamming the door behind him. In the kitchen, he hangs up the clothes as before and turns on the four electric rings. The front door buzzer sounds

Who's this? (*He goes to answer the intercom*) Yes?

Ruff's Voice Ruff here.

Reaper It's not too good up here.

Ruff's Voice Inspector Ruff. Is Mr Fogg there?

Reaper Um—sort of; rather whacked. Was it very important?

Fogg, his job finished, returns to the sitting-room and takes in what Ruff is saying

Ruff's Voice They found his car. Unfortunately, two men and a woman, seen running away from the car, have escaped, probably with the loot.

Fogg and Reaper freeze. A pause

Are you still there, sir?

Reaper Yes.

Ruff's Voice Then would you mind pushing the button? It's still pouring.

Reaper Yes, if I can find it. Just a sec. (*He cups the mouthpiece and hisses at Fogg*) Warn Di-Di. Tell her to keep mum. If he finds her he'll think she's the woman with the diamonds.

Fogg She *is* the woman with the diamonds.

Reaper Yes, but not the way he'll think she is, nit! He mustn't find her or the diamonds.

Fogg shrugs and heads to the bedroom. Reaper takes his hand off the mouth-piece

Sorry, Inspector. You can come up. I've found the button. You'll never guess where it was. (*To Fogg*) Where are the diamonds?
Fogg How should I know?

Reaper still holds off pressing the button. Fogg enters the bedroom, closing the door. Reaper presses the button and then starts a frantic search for the diamond packet. In the bedroom, Fogg knocks on the bathroom door

(*In a low voice*) Mrs—er—Diane. Danger. Not a sound.

Diane's head appears through the curtains. Fogg has his back to her. She walks out and taps him on the shoulder. He swings round with a gasp and his knees nearly give

Aaaaagh!
Diane I'm not in there. I'm here.
Fogg No! I thought you'd gone ages ago.
Diane I never got the chance. Besides . . .
Fogg This is terrible—and still half naked.
Diane Not the only one. (*She nudges him*) I saw your girl, sly old thing! Why did you call her Diane?
Fogg Because that's her name and she isn't—isn't mine, that is.

Fogg hastily pushes Diane behind the curtains as the bathroom door starts to open

Mrs Barker appears in the bathroom doorway

Mrs Barker Did you call me?
Fogg Yes. Ssssh! You must keep hidden. A detective's on his way up. You were spotted leaving the car and he thinks you're one of the crooks who stole those diamonds. (*He pushes her back*) Not a sound.

Mrs Barker disappears into the bathroom

Fogg closes the bathroom door. Diane looks out from the curtains

Diane Car? Crook? Diamonds?
Fogg No time to explain that. The money to pay your blackmail is under the pillow here. Put on some of my clothes and go out through this window.
Diane No. I must find my own clothes.
Fogg They are in the kitchen dustbin. They're no good to you.
Diane Yes, they are. My front door key's in one of the pockets.
Fogg Oh no! You couldn't have remembered before?
Diane I could have, but I didn't. It's no good my going without the key. Eddie would just find me on my doorstep wearing your clothes.

Fogg I'll—I'll try to get it. If I succeed, you go out through this window. Up the iron ladder and across the roof, turn to your right. Remember right all the time across to the house.

Diane is seen to be mentally experimenting to discover which is her right hand

Next door you'll find a skylight. It's always open because the kids are always playing there. Now, whatever you do, stay out of sight until I find your key!

Fogg runs out, closing the connecting door. Reaper is still searching the room desperately for the diamonds. Fogg heads towards the kitchen door

Reaper I can't find those ruddy diamonds anywhere. (*He grabs Fogg*) Where are you rushing to in such a hurry?
Fogg Key—in the dustbin . . .
Reaper Key?
Fogg Going to make some tea in the dustbin.

As Fogg tries to break away the front door opens

Ruff enters

Ruff Sorry to have been so long, gents. One of my men arrived with some new information on your car.
Reaper Oh? I've just been telling Fogg the good news about it.
Ruff *Good* news? (*To Fogg*) And were you pleased?
Fogg Er, yes. Yes.
Ruff Really?
Fogg (*back-tracking*) Well—quite pleased.
Ruff Really!
Fogg Well, fairly; not very. Shouldn't I be?
Ruff (*shrugging*) I don't know, sir. Some people get their pleasures in peculiar ways.
Reaper Yes, I could tell you about someone called Sybil.
Ruff Sybil? (*To Fogg*) By the way, sir, your car wasn't licensed. It was eight months out-of-date.
Fogg Oh. I'm terribly forgetful.
Ruff Certainly are. What with no insurance so not being able to make a claim . . .
Fogg Of course! You mean the accident . . .
Ruff (*sharply*) *What accident?*
Reaper Yes, what accident?
Fogg Didn't you say accident?
Ruff No. You did. There *was* one, but how did *you* know about it?
Reaper Yes, how did you know about it?
Fogg You said something about not making a claim.
Ruff And from that you *deduced* there had been an accident?
Fogg Yes.
Ruff Well deduced! Your car is a write-off.
Fogg Oh yes! Oh tut-tut-tut.

Ruff (*changing tack*) I can't help wondering if Mrs Barker, you remember, sir, your friend who was kidnapped in your car, I can't help wondering if Mrs Barker and the woman who ran away from the car aren't one and the same.

Fogg How can you possibly assume that the lady who ran away from the car is a member of the gang?

Ruff (*sharply*) Because a nice, innocent girl who had been kidnapped and then escaped would have rushed straight round to the police by now and reported it, wouldn't she?

Reaper Good point. Well taken.

Fogg Anyway, I'm absolutely certain Diane Barker knew nothing about the theft of diamonds.

Reaper⎫
Ruff ⎭ *What diamonds?*⎰ (*Speaking together*)

Reaper Keats!

Ruff Shelley. (*To Fogg*) What diamonds?

Reaper Yes, what diamonds?

Fogg (*floundering*) Didn't you say diamonds?

Ruff No, you did.

Fogg Ah—ah—ah! Well, if it was the Quiet Gang it would be diamonds, wouldn't it? Er—was it?

Ruff (*grimly*) I don't know if it was the Quiet Gang or not. It was certainly diamonds. So, well deduced again.

Reaper Has the robbery been reported yet?

Ruff No, it hasn't, but these loose stones—(*he produces some loose diamonds from his pocket*)—were found in the back of Mr Fogg's car.

Reaper (*looking at them*) Nice stones.

Ruff You're the expert, sir. You couldn't tell me where these stones came from?

Reaper Yes.

Ruff (*eagerly*) Where?

Reaper The back of Mr Fogg's car.

Ruff (*grimly*) Thanks. (*He pockets the diamonds*) Well, so far, all we have is a good description of the mystery lady and what she was wearing.

Reaper (*in a hollow voice*) Oh!

Ruff Blonde, in her twenties, wearing blue slacks and a multi-coloured top. Shouldn't be difficult to trace with a description like that.

Behind Ruff's back Fogg agitatedly waves his hand at Reaper, indicating that the tell-tale clothes are in the kitchen. Ruff suddenly turns, and catches him at it. Fogg then pretends to be catching a fly. He chases it with his hands, finally "kills" it by clapping his hands together, then flicks it on to the floor. Ruff, not fooled at all, grinds the imaginary fly into the carpet. Playing along, Reaper takes out his jeweller's eye-glass, fits it in his eye, takes out a pair of tweezers, lifts Ruff's foot, extracts the supposedly squashed fly off Ruff's sole, then carries it away upstage. At this moment there is the deafening clamour of the burglar alarm. Fogg switches it off

Reaper That *is* a break-in! After them, Inspector!

Ruff No, wait a minute. This time you two can help me with my enquiries. (*He pushes Fogg and Reaper ahead of him to the shop door*)

Fogg, Reaper and Ruff exit

Diane emerges from behind the curtain

Simultaneously, the bathroom door opens and Mrs Barker, dripping and "wrapped" in a minute hand-towel, comes out

Mrs Barker Oooh!
Diane Oh, hello! You're Foggy's friend.
Mrs Barker Yes, who are you?
Diane Diane Reaper.
Mrs Barker Funny, my name's Diane, too. You Eddie Reaper's wife?
Diane Yes.
Mrs Barker What was that awful clanging?
Diane Burglar alarm. May be my chance to have one more crack at trying to find my clothes and key.
Mrs Barker What happened to your clothes?
Diane They've disappeared ever since Foggy took them off me.
Mrs Barker *Foggy* took off your clothes?

Diane peeks through the keyhole, unaware of Mrs Barker's suspicious looks

Diane Yes. (*She turns back*) If I don't reappear, tell Foggy I've gone, at last.
Mrs Barker (*more and more puzzled*) You do mean *Foggy*, not your husband?
Diane Oh yes! Don't tell my husband whatever you do. He mustn't know I was here.
Mrs Barker Look, what's between Foggy and you?
Diane Don't worry! We're just good friends. (*She slips out and crosses the sitting-room*)
Mrs Barker I don't like the sound of *that*.

Mrs Barker goes back into the bathroom, closing the door

Diane enters the kitchen and starts a renewed search for her clothes. She finally locates them in the waste-bin. She reacts in dismay at their condition, but rescues her key from the pocket. She notices Mrs Barker's clothes drying above the stove. She hesitates a second, then decides to take them. She switches off the electric rings. She quickly slips on the top, and then the trousers. These are too tight and split open as she pulls them on (Velcro). She goes back to the bedroom, takes the money from under the pillow of the bed, then moves to the window and starts practising left from right

Diane Left—right . . .

Carrying the key and money in her hand, Diane climbs out of the window, bumping her head in the process, and exits

The alarm bell goes off as Diane exits

Reaper charges in through the shop door

With a curse he halts, turns to the control board and furiously starts throwing switches this way and that. The alarm still rings. He aims a kick at it, and it mysteriously stops. He reacts, then runs through the connecting door, across the bedroom, and bangs on the bathroom door

Reaper Di-Di! Come out!

Mrs Barker, inadequately wrapped as ever, appears in the bathroom doorway. She wears panties but no bra, and covers her chest with the small towel

Oh, what a waste! What a waste! Quick! Now, there's a chance for you to get out of here now, while the Inspector is down below. Go out through the kitchen window when we've got your clothes. (*He starts to pull her out*)
Mrs Barker Half a mo! My bra.

Mrs Barker returns to the bathroom

Reaper thinks about her, and warms his hands over the double lamp expressively

Reaper I thought you girls had abandoned bras.

Mrs Barker reappears, doing up her bra. He has to assist her, delaying them further

Mrs Barker Some of us lucky ones *have* to wear them. Did you have a burglary?
Reaper Yes, a cat burglary.
Mrs Barker You caught a cat burglar?
Reaper No, a cat. My partner's cat fell down the bloody chimney and set the alarm off. Breathe in a bit. (*He struggles*) You'll never make a jockey. (*He leads her through the connecting door and across the sitting-room*)
Mrs Barker What's your partner's cat doing *here*? In your flat?
Reaper Um—popped in for a pinta. He's not getting enough. I know just how he feels. I say, you don't know what happened to that parcel of diamonds, do you?
Mrs Barker Yes. I put them in my trousers pocket.
Reaper I wish you'd told me before. I've been going spare, looking for them.

Reaper and Mrs Barker enter the kitchen

Shove on your gear, then, and give me the diamonds.
Mrs Barker Where are my things?

Reaper gives a big reaction as he sees the clothes are missing from above the stove

Reaper They were *there*! Where are they?

Mrs Barker *I* don't know. I never saw them after Eddie Reaper took them off to dry them. Here, talking of girls taking off their clothes, Foggy . . .

Reaper I don't want to talk about any other clothes but yours. You've got to get out of here. Ah, the oven! (*He dives for the oven and opens it. Relief. The clothes are not there*)

Mrs Barker (*with a giggle*) He wouldn't put them in the oven, silly!

Reaper Want to bet? Where the hell are they?

Mrs Barker Why not ask Eddie Reaper?

Reaper Because Eddie Reaper's down below trying to get the cat out of the chimney. (*Searching*) Hell! Why can't he leave things . . . (*He opens the cupboard door, gestures to her*) Keep out of sight. We'll have to wait until I can corner the foul Fogg and find out where he hid them. (*He pushes her towards the cupboard*)

Mrs Barker Why do you call Eddie Reaper "Fogg"?

Reaper (*with one blink*) Not "Fogg", dear, "Frog". He's of Frrrrench extrrrraction.

Mrs Barker I like the way you roll your Rs.

Reaper I like the way you roll yours, too.

Reaper pushes Mrs Barker in, and closes the door, then goes into the sitting-room. He continues the search for the clothes and enters the bedroom, leaving the door open

The window in the kitchen opens and Diane's leg comes through. She drops on to the sink and clambers to the floor, still carrying the money and key in her hand, then goes into the sitting-room

Reaper has his back to Diane as he looks about the bedroom. Diane stops dead as she sees Reaper, then dashes back to the kitchen, closing the door behind her. The sound of the door attracts Reaper's notice. He looks puzzled

Diane hastily climbs out through the kitchen window again

Reaper enters the kitchen, and is just in time to see the last of Diane's legs disappearing through the window

Reaper Hey! Di-Di, you found your clothes, then? Come back! You forgot to give me the diamonds! Di-Di! Di-Di!

Mrs Barker looks out of the cupboard

Mrs Barker (*very loudly*) What?

Reaper Aaagh! You! But—(*he looks at the window*)—there's a fella just like you went out on to the roof. Get back in there.

Mrs Barker retreats into the cupboard, closing the door. Reaper climbs up on the sink, opens the window and starts to climb through

Ruff and Fogg enter through the shop door

Ruff runs into the kitchen, followed by Fogg. Ruff is in time to see Reaper's legs disappearing through the window. Ruff reaches up, takes hold of Reaper's legs and pulls him back, turning him and carrying him back, causing him some pain

Oooh! That was my loose change!

Ruff Not trying to escape, are you, sir?

Reaper (*angrily*) Escape? From what? No, I saw someone climbing through this window. I might have caught them, but for you.

Ruff climbs on to the sink

Ruff Let's have a look, then. (*To Fogg*) Shove on those outside lights of yours, sir.

Fogg Oh, no—yes—all right.

Ruff (*to Reaper*) You might come too, sir. Four eyes are better than two.

Fogg Even shifty ones like yours.

Ruff hastily pulls himself through the window

Reaper prepares to follow, but first hisses at Fogg

Reaper Di-Di's shirt and slacks. Where are they?

Fogg I don't know.

Reaper Find them.

Fogg What shall I do with them if I find them?

Reaper Hide them.

Fogg What's the point of that if they're already hidden?

Reaper So *I* can find them again, nit!

Ruff's head appears through the window

Ruff (*to Reaper*) Aren't you joining me, sir? And careful of your loose change climbing through.

Ruff's head disappears again. Reaper grumblingly climbs on the sink and out of the window

Fogg goes to the sitting-room, then to the connecting door and looks into the bedroom

Fogg Diane? Have you gone?

No answer. Looking greatly relieved, Fogg moves back into the kitchen. He takes the second pie from the refrigerator and puts it in the oven, which he switches on. He hums quite happily to himself

Simultaneously, Diane climbs back through the bedroom window and draws the curtains closed behind her. Suddenly she discovers that she

*is no longer carrying the key or the money. She lets out a mournful cry
of woe*

*Fogg leaves the kitchen, crosses the sitting-room, and goes through the
connecting door to the bedroom just as Diane turns back towards the
window*

Fogg Oh, no!
Diane Hello, Foggy!
Fogg What do you mean, "Hello"? I thought you'd got away.
Diane I did, but somehow I landed back through your kitchen skylight.
Fogg You turned left instead of right, didn't you?
Diane I expect so. I generally do.
Fogg This wasn't the time to do it, damn it! (*With sudden horror*) And
those clothes! Take them off at once.
Diane Why?
Fogg Because the police suspect they belong to a crook. Their descrip-
tion's been circulated all over London.

*Diane sighs and starts to strip. Fogg takes jeans and a sweater from the
built-in cupboard*

Diane And there's something else, Foggy.
Fogg If it's bad news I don't want to hear it.
Diane It is. I must have dropped my key and the money outside on the
roof.
Fogg NO! Oh my God! (*He looks up at the ceiling, fearing the worst is
happening above*)
Diane We'll find them. They're out there somewhere, near the kitchen
window, I think.
Fogg And so are Eddie and that detective! If *they* find them, that's it.
We've had it.

*Simultaneously, Diane begins to weep and, outside, it starts to pelt with rain
harder than ever before*

(*Irritably*) Oh, spare me the waterworks.

Reaper's voice is heard off

Reaper (*off*) We'll get drowned. Back through the bedroom window.
Fogg Bedroom window! (*He gives a muted yelp, dives his hand through the
curtains and locks the window*) Have you any idea where you dropped
the key and money?
Diane I tripped and fell just outside the kitchen window when I went out
the second time.
Fogg All right. Now, I'm going to try and get Eddie and the detective out
of the way for a few minutes.
Diane How?
Fogg Doesn't matter how. If I succeed I'll go out and look for the key
and money. Meanwhile, stay hidden in the bathroom, get dressed and
be ready to leave at a moment's notice. (*He picks up Mrs Barker's top
and pants, and indicates the jeans and sweater*)

Diane (*tearfully*) Yes. I'm sorry I'm such a nuisance.
Fogg So am I.

Reaper and Ruff bang on the window

Reaper (*off*) Damn and blast! Fogg! Open up!
Ruff (*off*) Open this window!

Diane hastily exits to the bathroom, taking the sweater and jeans

Fogg leaves the bedroom, crosses the sitting-room and enters the kitchen. His first act is to close and lock the kitchen window. Next he opens the broom cupboard door and hurls Mrs Barker's clothes inside—and smack into Mrs Barker's face since he does not realize she is in there. She utters an angry, startled cry, and comes out. There is more banging on the bedroom window

Fogg Aaaagh! Oh, it's you.
Mrs Barker My clothes! Just look at them.
Fogg I should forget them. They're red hot.
Mrs Barker They're sopping. How can I go home like that?
Fogg No idea. I've other things to worry about. (*He goes into the sitting-room*)
Mrs Barker (*offended*) Charming!
Reaper (*off*) Back the way we came. Kitchen window.

Mrs Barker begins to hang the clothes on the line above the stove. She turns on the electric rings. In the sitting-room Fogg is working fast. First he opens a drawer and takes out a torch, which he pockets. From another drawer he takes out a reel of black cotton. He ties a loop in the end of the cotton and attaches this to one of the switches on the alarm control board. Then he carefully lays a trail of cotton along the floor and through the connecting door into the bedroom. He finally places the reel on the bedroom table

Reaper appears at the kitchen window. Finding it locked he lets out a yell of rage

Mrs Barker hares back into the cupboard again

Reaper (*outside the window*) What the hell! Let us in!

Ruff joins Reaper outside the kitchen window

Fogg, who has not yet finished the actions described above, continues calmly about his work, totally ignoring the thumps and cries

Ruff (*outside the window*) Open up!
Reaper (*outside the window*) Do you want us to drown? Open this window!

Fogg now enters the kitchen and moves to a position near the window on which Ruff and Reaper are hammering. The ensuing conversation is conducted in loud shouts

Fogg Hullo. Something up?

Reaper (*outside the window*) You want to leave us here all night?

Fogg Yes. Everything's all right. How's it out there?

Reaper (*outside the window*) OPEN THIS BLOODY WINDOW OR I'LL SMASH IT!

Fogg climbs up and turns the bolt. The window opens, and Reaper is the first to come through, literally dripping

What are you playing at?

Fogg The catch must have slipped.

Reaper Your mother must have slipped!

Reaper sees Mrs Barker's much-wanted clothes drying above the stove. He gives a strangled cry and looks up at the window, where Ruff is coming through backwards and feet first. In a swift, panic move Reaper seizes the clothes off the line, opens the oven door and hurls the clothes inside the oven. He slams the oven door shut a second before Ruff comes through and looks down. Reaper switches off the electric rings

Ruff I thought I told you to put those outside lights on.

Fogg I did but a bluse fude.

Ruff A what!

Fogg A bluse fuu. Did you—er—discover anything out there?

Reaper fiercely slaps his jacket pocket, and a large jet of water shoots out. (This is a specially prepared pocket)

Reaper Yes. A slight drizzle.

Fogg Look out, you're doing it all over my wall, and you're making pa, pa, pu, puddles.

Reaper Anyone would make pa, pa, puddles if they were locked out in the middle of the monsoon.

Fogg goes into the sitting-room. Ruff and Reaper follow him

Ruff Mr Fogg. Mr Fogg, are you hard of hearing?

Fogg Pardon?

Ruff You didn't hear us bashing on the windows and yelling to be let in?

Fogg No. Well, yes, just now, when I did let you in.

Reaper What were you doing while we were out there?

Fogg That's my business.

Reaper Pretty noisy business, not to have heard the din we were making.

Fogg (*coldly*) I happened to be in the bathroom. And I hadn't quite finished, so if you'll excuse me . . . (*To Ruff*) I take it I have your permission to use my bathroom?

Ruff Is he deaf?

Reaper Pardon?

Fogg goes through the connecting door into the bedroom, closing it after

*him. He picks up the cotton, draws it taut, then gives a good tug. The switch
on the board turns down and the main alarm clangs off. The rain stops*

Ruff Oh Gawd! There we go again! Come on, sir. It can't be pussy this
time.

Ruff drags Reaper through the shop door, where they exit

*Fogg goes to the bedroom window, unlocks the catch and looks out before
drawing the curtains again and moving to the bathroom door, which he opens
a little*

Fogg It's stopped raining. I'm going to find the money and the key now.

Diane's head appears in the doorway

Diane Thanks, Foggy.
Fogg Somewhere near the kitchen window, you said?

Diane nods

Keep out of sight.

Diane disappears back into the bathroom

*He closes the bathroom door, goes from the bedroom across the sitting-room
to the kitchen*

*He climbs up and out through the kitchen window, where he is seen
looking around outside. He utters a satisfied exclamation and bends down,
disappearing, to reappear again almost immediately*

Got it!

Reaper enters through the shop door and heads for the kitchen

Fogg starts to return, legs first, backwards through the window

Reaper (*towards the broom cupboard*) Patience, my love. We'll be rid of
Sherlock soon.

*Fogg's legs give a convulsive jerk and he starts to get out of the window
again. Reaper hears something, sees the legs, and makes a dive at them.
He grabs the legs but only succeeds in pulling Fogg's trousers right off.
Reaper falls backwards to the floor*

Fogg's trouserless legs disappear through the window

Reaper rises, climbs up and starts to climb out of the window

Come back, you!

*Ruff enters through the shop door, goes into the kitchen and, exactly as
before, sees Reaper's legs disappearing through the window*

Ruff seizes Reaper's legs and, as before, drags him back, with the same painful results. He sets Reaper on to the ground

Reaper Oooh! That was *not* my small change.
Ruff Where were you off to this time, sir?
Reaper I nearly caught someone going out that window. Either a man, or a woman with hairy legs.
Ruff An ape, perhaps?
Reaper I'm not lying, for once.
Ruff For once?
Reaper For twice, then. Look! I pulled these trousers off him!

Fogg enters the bedroom through the bedroom window, minus his trousers, in a breathless panic. He closes the curtains

While Ruff climbs up and looks out of the kitchen window, Fogg rushes to the wardrobe, finds a similar-looking pair of trousers and pulls them on hastily

Ruff Let's have a look, then. Which way did he go?
Reaper Through the window and over the roof. To the right.

Reaper looks suspiciously at the trousers, recognizing them. Ruff climbs down and also reacts to the trousers

Ruff No-one in sight. (*Noting the trousers*) You took these off him, did you? Good work, good work. Invaluable.
Reaper Fingerprints?
Ruff I've seen these before. Where's your disappearing chum, then?

Fogg runs to the bathroom door, opens it, and throws the key into the bathroom

Fogg (*in a whisper*) Here's your key. I still haven't got the money. I lost it with my trousers. I'll try to get it back. (*He closes the bathroom door and runs to the connecting door*)

Ruff enters the sitting-room from the kitchen

Ruff Mr Fogg! Mr Fogg!

Fogg enters the sitting-room through the connecting door, doing his best to appear nonchalant

Fogg You called?
Ruff (*clearly put out to see him*) Oh! Where have you been?
Fogg In the bathroom. I've finished.
Ruff I bet that's a relief. That one should go down in the *Guinness Book of Records*. (*He circles Fogg suspiciously, looking closely at his trousers*)

In the kitchen, Reaper has discovered the wad of money in the other trousers' pocket. Mrs Barker emerges from the cupboard close to him

Mrs Barker (*in a whisper*) What's that?
Reaper (*in a whisper*) Money.

Mrs Barker Can I have it?

Reaper No, you can't. It's not yours. It's got someone else's picture on it. (*He pushes her back into the cupboard, closes the door and moves away*) And these are Foggy's pants. (*He puts the money into his own hip pocket and goes into the sitting-room carrying the trousers. He looks at Fogg's trousers, and then at the trousers in his hand*) What the . . . How the . . .?

Fogg has his eyes glued nervously on the trousers in Reaper's hand. Ruff walks to Reaper and takes the trousers from him. Fogg looks appalled. Ruff approaches Fogg and holds out the trousers

Ruff (*to Reaper*) May I? (*To Fogg*) Are these yours?

Fogg I—er—don't think so.

Ruff They look remarkably like the ones you were wearing.

Fogg That I *am* wearing, you mean. Yes, they do. Can I have a closer look?

Ruff hands Fogg the trousers

Ruff By all means.

Fogg makes quite a business of examining the trousers

Fogg Same colour and weight, but a different make, I think . . . (*He contrives to turn away while apparently looking closely for a maker's name-tag. As he does this he feels desperately into the hip pocket for the wad of notes. Empty. His face falls and he freezes temporarily*) No. Definitely not mine. (*He turns back*) They belong to somebody called St Michael.

Ruff They were left behind by someone who nipped out on to the roof. You, sir?

Fogg You're getting muddled. It's you that's been out on the roof, not me.

Reaper Whoever was wearing those trousers was on the roof, because I pulled them off him as he just went out.

Fogg Oh? He'll be feeling rather chilly, then, out there with no trousers.

Ruff gives Fogg a look, then walks to the connecting door and glances through into the bedroom, which appears empty. He is about to come back again when something catches his eye. He enters the bedroom and picks up the reel of cotton. He comes back, feeling his way along the length of cotton until he stops near the alarm control board where the cotton ends

Ruff Herhmmm mm, at last! A lead. All sorts of possibilities here.

Reaper looks puzzled. Fogg is frozen. Ruff turns and looks steadily at Fogg, who tries a smile but fails

Reaper What is that?

Ruff What's this? It's a length of black cotton, sir, with a loop on the end.

Fogg Oh, that's mine. I was—er—sewing on a button.

Ruff Fifteen feet of cotton to sew on a button?

Fogg If a job's worth doing it's worth doing well. (*Lamely*) That's what I always say. What do you always say?

Ruff Where's the button?

Fogg I didn't need it; I found it was a zip.

Ruff Mr Fogg, when you were doing whatever you were doing in the bathroom just now the burglar alarm went off.

Fogg Yes.

Ruff You didn't ask us what it was?

Fogg What it was . . . Oh, what was it?

Ruff It was nothing we could discover. Nothing was disturbed in the shop, and pussy's in the corridor.

Fogg I'll write to the makers. It must have gone off by itself.

Ruff There is another way it *could* have gone off.

Fogg Oh?

Ruff If you'd attached this cotton to the switch and tugged it from inside the bedroom.

Fogg Why should I do a thing like that?

Ruff To get me out of this flat and downstairs again.

Fogg Pre—pre—pre . . .

Ruff Preposterous?

Fogg Precisely.

Ruff Maybe; but would you mind if I aired a little theory to you gents, among friends?

Reaper Feel free.

Ruff Thank you. I think you two and a woman called Diane Barker used Mr Fogg's car in the course of a jewel robbery which went wrong.

Reaper What!

Fogg How dare you! We are established jewellers.

Ruff Established car dealers have been known to trade in hot cars.

Fogg You have not one shred of evidence to convict us of any crime.

Ruff (*producing the diamonds*) I have these five loose stones found in your car, for a start! Are they yours?

Fogg No.

Ruff Fine; then that's five shreds of evidence for a start. I think they fell out of a stone parcel of diamonds and that the parcel, and possibly some cash, are hidden somewhere in this flat.

Fogg Pure supposition.

Ruff The Quiet Gang concentrate on diamonds and cash.

Fogg The Quiet Gang! Us!

Reaper (*laughing*) Us the Quiet Gang! That's rich!

Ruff So are they. Have you any objections if I searched the flat?

Reaper Yes! You don't search without a warrant.

Ruff I'll get one.

Reaper No, I don't think you will—because you don't even know if a robbery has been committed yet.

Ruff (*showing the diamonds*) There must have been. Look at these stones

Reaper But has anyone actually *reported* a robbery?

Ruff (*defensively*) Not yet, but . . .

Reaper Very well. Suppose we say these stones *do* belong to us?

Ruff He said they didn't.

Reaper Supposing he changes his mind?

Fogg How can you prove they aren't ours?
Reaper Yes. We're jewellers. We keep a lot of stones in our oven.
Ruff In your *oven*?
Reaper Oven? Did you say oven? Who keeps diamonds in an oven?

Mention of ovens suddenly reminds Fogg of something

Fogg Oh my goodness! I forgot. (*He moves towards the kitchen*)
Ruff Where are you going?
Fogg I put a pie in the safe! I mean oven. (*He goes into the kitchen*)

Ruff is tempted to follow Fogg, but Reaper lays a hand on his arm

Reaper Inspector, you're barking up the wrong tree, and remember, there's such a thing as wrongful arrest.
Ruff Nobody's been arrested *yet*, Mr Reaper.

Reaper sits down, feeling the strain. In the kitchen, Fogg goes straight towards the oven to deal with his pie. The cupboard door opens a little, and Mrs Barker's voice, strained, is heard. She cannot be seen

Mrs Barker (*inside the cupboard*) Water. Parched. Roasting in here.
Fogg Yes, it is. Whew! (*He whispers*) You'll have to hang on, I'm afraid. Don't come out. He hasn't gone yet. I'll get you some water.

Fogg moves to the sink, picks up a glass and fills it with water from the tap. At the same time Ruff, suspicious, tiptoes, unseen by Fogg, into the kitchen doorway and stands watching. Fogg, his back to Ruff, hands the glass into the cupboard. His arm disappears for a moment, then returns minus the glass. Ruff claps his hands appreciatively

Ruff That was clever! The way you made that glass disappear in that cupboard.

Fogg whirls round, mouth open

Could you bring it back again? Go on, have a go.

Fogg miserably raises his arm and lets it disappear into the cupboard again. It reappears almost instantly, with the glass still filled with water

Yes, you've done it! Marvellous! How do you do it?
Fogg No, no. I mustn't tell you; I'm a member of the Magic Circle.
Ruff Once again. Please! For me. I may never see this trick again.

Fogg realizes he is being toyed with, but carries on. He repeats the process and then withdraws his arm, minus the glass

It's gone, it's gone! Once more. Once again. The last time.

Fogg again repeats the process, and this time produces the glass, which no longer contains any water and is upside down

Look at that! Upside down as well! Marvellous! Do you think I could have a go?
Fogg No! No! No!

Fogg tries to close the cupboard, but Ruff gently pushes him aside

Ruff I insist. Are you watching closely, sir? Nothing in my hands. Nothing up my sleeve. Could I borrow the glass? I wonder if I've got the knack. One, two—(*he feels something in the cupboard*)—*two!* Ouch!

Reaper enters the kitchen and gives a horrified start, then a murderous look at Fogg. Ruff gently pulls Mrs Barker out into the kitchen in her bra and pants

Look at this! The jackpot! (*To Fogg*) I've done even better than you. Shall I saw her in half, or will you?

Reaper forces an extremely forced laugh

Reaper Ha! Ha! Ha! (*To Fogg*) Why didn't you tell us Brigitte was here?

Mrs Barker and Fogg react. Ruff listens and watches like a lynx

Fogg Brigitte?
Ruff Bridget who, sir?
Reaper (*with French pronunciation*) Brigitt-*eu*. Inspect-*eu*, Brigitte is a *bonne amie* of old Fo . . . of my partner. May I present the *Contesse de le Touquet*. Brigitte, *je vous presente l'Inspecteur* Ruff, another *bon ami* of ours. (*Sotto voce*) She speaks very little English.
Ruff (*playing along*) Charmed, *Contesse*. (*Speaking very distinctly*) This may seem a stupid question, but were you doing anything terribly important in zee broom cupboard just now?
Mrs Barker (*very English*) Pardon?
Ruff Um—what—were you doing in the cupboard of the broom?
Reaper She's desperately shy—(*sotto voce to Ruff*)—and she's also married, so *fermez la bouche, s'il vous plait.*
Ruff Understood. Quite a one for the marrieds, isn't he, that one? (*To Mrs Barker*) Shall we retreat *dans la salon, Contessa. Dans la salon?* (*To Reaper*) Are you coming, sir?

Ruff leads Mrs Barker past Reaper and into the sitting-room. Reaper approaches Fogg and does a little piece of ventriloquism

Reaper You stukid gugger!

Reaper and Fogg, who has again forgotten his pie, follow Ruff and Mrs Barker into the sitting-room

Ruff Bit nippy; perhaps the Countess would like to put on some clothes.
Reaper (*quickly*) No, she hasn't any clothes.
Ruff None at all?
Reaper She's a nudist.
Ruff Well, hardly. (*He looks at Mrs Barker as if saying, "Well, hardly a nudist"*)
Fogg A nearly nudist.
Ruff Does she live here?
Fogg } No. Yes. } (*Speaking together*)
Reaper } Yes. No. }
Ruff Yes and no, eh?
Fogg On and off.

Ruff More off than on, by the look of it.
Reaper Please! Inspector! A *petite delicatessen*! *S'il vous plait!*
Ruff I'm referring to her accommodation, sir, not to how accommodating
the Countess might be. (*To Mrs Barker*) So, sometimes you're here and
sometimes you're not?

Mrs Barker nods

Now, when you're not here, *ici*, but decide to come here, *ici*, you come
from there, wherever "there" may be. Where is that?
Reaper The *Château de le Touquet*. The *Contesse de le Touquet* lives in the
Château de le Touquet at . . .
Ruff Le Touquet?
Reaper *Boulogne.*
Ruff (*to Fogg*) So the *Contesse de le Touquet* leaves the *Château de le
Touquet* at Boulogne and comes here.
Fogg Sometimes.
Ruff Dressed like that?
Reaper *Always.*
Fogg Summer and winter.
Ruff No trouble at Customs, then. Presumably she heads for the green
light saying "Nothing to Declare".

*Ruff stretches his arms wide and does a fancy walk. Reaper looks at him,
raises his eyebrows and turns to Fogg. Mrs Barker discreetly covers her top
which is threatening to become exposed*

Reaper (*to Fogg*) There's a lot of it about, Sybil. (*To Ruff*) Well, nothing
dutiable.
Ruff (*like a whiplash*) What about passports?
Fogg Day trips only. None needed.
Ruff H'm. Do you know what *I* think?

No-one ventures an answer

I think we have the little gang all together at last. Now all we have to
do is locate a striped shirt and blue pants, a packet or two of diamonds
and maybe some cash.

A tinny, continuous (male) voice is heard. Reactions from all

Tinny Voice Garble, garble.
Reaper Someone got a parrot?

Ruff produces a radio

Ruff Ruff here. Over.
Tinny Voice Garble, garble . . .

The completely unintelligible voice continues for some moments

Ruff Understood. Well, gentlemen, if you'll excuse me . . .
Reaper Before you go, Inspector, I have a confession to make.

Ruff looks keenly interested

Ruff Just in time, sir. What?

Reaper I've grown exceedingly tired of your face.

Ruff I've been tired of it for years.

Reaper But *you* have to look at it and we don't.

Ruff Is that a way of telling me I'm not welcome any more?

Reaper You're quick. I can see how you've come so far. I suggest you stay away from this flat until you have a warrant or something of positive interest to discuss.

Ruff (*agreeably*) Very well put, sir. And within your rights. By the way, Squad Car Four, who called me up just now, was at the scene of the accident. They must have found something new to report.

Reaper (*quickly*) What?

Ruff Who knows, sir? I'll pop back if it proves of positive interest. Perhaps you'd like to escort me down through the shop. That alarm is beginning to terrify me.

Reaper (*picking up Ruff's hat*) Votre chapeau.

Ruff *Merci.*

Reaper After you, Inspector.

Ruff exits through the shop door

Fogg I'd give up if I were you. Make a clean breast of the whole thing before it's too late.

Reaper No! He's still bluffing. He's got no proof. So bite on the bullet, put the bit between the teeth and hang on. It suits me to go below. I can put this thousand quid I found in the mystery pants in the money safe for the time being.

Fogg No, no, no.

Ruff reappears through the shop door

Ruff Are you coming, Mr Reaper? I've got other cases to deal with besides this one, you know.

Reaper starts to move forward with a nod

Ruff exits again

Reaper suddenly halts and turns to Fogg

Reaper Well? You heard what the man said.

Fogg Yes. He said, "Are you coming, Mr Reaper?"

Reaper (*meaningly*) Yes. *Mister Reaper*. Are *you* coming downstairs.

Fogg (*furiously*) Augh!

Fogg exits through the shop door

Reaper That partner of mine knows more about that money than he makes out. I'll swear that was him getting on to the roof. But why? Why? I can check in the safe, but he wouldn't be nicking it. He's deplorably honest.

Mrs Barker Poor little Reaper. I feel rather sorry for him. (*She nuzzles close and puts her arm round him*) Are we going to get away with it . . . (*She reacts*) Here, you are *sopping*, Foggy. Get changed.

Reaper I'll wait till I get home.

Mrs Barker You *are* home.

Reaper (*hastily*) Of course I'm home. I mean I'll wait till *they've* gone home.

Mrs Barker You'll do no such thing. Get into your bedroom and get those clothes off. You'll catch your death of cold.

Reaper has no option but to agree. He enters the bedroom. Mrs Barker follows him in. He removes his jacket and shirt

Oh, talking of people taking their clothes off reminds me. His wife has gone.

Reaper Who's wife?

Mrs Barker Eddie Reaper's wife. She was hiding in here with hardly any clothes on—as if you didn't know.

Reaper Reaper's wife—was here—with hardly any clothes on?

Mrs Barker She told me to tell you she'd gone but on no account to let Eddie know she'd been here.

Reaper stands with his trousers still on

Reaper Who said she was Eddie Reaper's wife?

Mrs Barker She did, of course.

Reaper She did. And you say she's gone?

Mrs Barker Yes. She said, "Tell Foggy I've gone at last but whatever you do don't tell my husband I was here." Something like that. Odd, isn't it?

Reaper (*his voice a little shaky*) Very odd. Um—what did she look like?

Mrs Barker Blonde. Good figure. About twenty-five. Funny, isn't it, she's called Diane, too.

Reaper (*in a yell*) DIANE!

Behind them, unseen, the bathroom door fleetingly opens and Diane, now dressed, looks out, opens her mouth in a silent cry, then closes the door again

Mrs Barker Yes—and *don't* tell me you're just good friends.

Reaper starts visibly to twitch. He removes his trousers and starts to strangle them. He pulls them inside out. Quite beside himself, he puts his arms through the legs, then pulls the trousers over his head, temporarily blinding himself

Mrs Barker What on earth are you doing?

She helps him out of the mess. He now puts the trousers back on his legs, but inside out and back to front, so that the zip is at the back

Reaper She was here all the time—under my nose—fool—explains everything . . .

Mrs Barker Are you all right?

Reaper Yes, I'm fine. Why?

Mrs Barker Your face is twitching.

Reaper (*twitching hard*) Fine. Cool as cauliflower—cucumber—ice—cold
—killer—kill him.

Fogg, looking nervous, enters through the shop door

Fogg I say!

*Reaper, hearing Fogg's voice, lets forth a snarl and lurches forward, holding
up the trousers which constantly threaten to fall*

Reaper (*to Mrs Barker*) Stay here. I have a little personal business to discuss. (*He goes through the connecting door, slamming it*) Seducer!

Fogg Ah! I don't know what you mean.

Reaper I only know one reason for a wife visiting her husband's partner
and stripping off in his bedroom.

Fogg There could be two!

Reaper (*triumphantly*) Ah! Then you admit Diane was here?

Fogg (*feeling a little hope*) Was?

Reaper Yes! You helped her to escape through the kitchen window and
I nearly caught her—and you. (*He twitches*) You know what you've
done? You've destroyed my faith in human nature, Fogg. I was a starry-
eyed idealist until I trod in you.

Fogg You! Ho!

Reaper You dirty Fogg you! You dirty, foul, thick Fogg. How could you
do this to me? Your friend and partner. And here I have been all
evening trying to get you out of trouble. I don't blame Diane. She
could always be led astray—like posing for those nude magazine pictures
a few years back.

Fogg You knew about that?

Reaper Yes. Of course I did. I've always known.

Fogg Oh, I'm relieved to hear that, Eddie . . .

Reaper (*in a fury again*) You've no cause to be relieved about anything.
You've shattered my life. You know what I was going to do a few
minutes ago? I decided to kill myself.

Fogg Oh, no!

Reaper But I changed my mind.

Fogg Thank goodness.

Reaper (*advancing*) I'm going to kill you instead.

*Reaper grabs Fogg by the throat. Fogg lets out a strangled yell which brings
Mrs Barker in from the bedroom. She tries to drag Fogg away. His head
lands in her cleavage. Reaper grapples with Fogg and his trousers fall down.
This is the tableau presented to Ruff as he comes in*

Ruff enters through the shop door

Ruff Well, well! Is this a Ladies' Excuse Me, or can I join in?

Reaper releases Fogg, whose head remains glued in Mrs Barker's cleavage

Reaper Sorry, Inspector. I was just showing him a little karate. Hai! Hai! (*He gives Fogg a tremendous back-hander in the nether regions*) Hai!

Fogg's eyes roll. He clasps himself and collapses on the sofa in agony. Reaper moves to the connecting door to the bedroom, carrying his trousers

Now sing *The Sound of Music*! (*He goes into the bedroom, leaves his trousers, borrows Fogg's dressing-gown and returns almost immediately*)

Ruff (*to Fogg*) Have I got a little surprise for you, sir.

Fogg (*in a falsetto*) A nice surprise, I hope.

Ruff Depends on how you look at it. Another little something found in the back of your car.

Reaper Something disgusting, I'll bet, by what goes on here.

Ruff No, but interesting. (*He produces a lady's handbag with the initials D.B. on it*)

Reaper raises his eyebrows, looking at Ruff and the handbag. Mrs Barker gives a little gasp

Reaper Very nice. Suits you.

Ruff One lady's handbag. Recognize it, *Contesse*?

Reaper No. She doesn't carry a handbag.

Ruff (*pointing*) With the initials "D.B.". Now what could they stand for?

Reaper Dirty Basket!

Ruff Or Diane Barker?

Reaper By George! You're right. It must belong to the girl who's missing.

Ruff You should have been a detective, sir! Now, what have we inside? (*Producing a nightie*) Look at this! One lady's nightie.

Reaper And that's all!

Ruff Not quite all, sir. (*He takes out a gold locket on a chain*) One gold locket containing a wedding photograph.

Mrs Barker looks horrified. Reaper glares at Mrs Barker. Ruff looks at Fogg

Would you care to take a guess at the identity of the happy couple? Go on. No prizes for guessing who the blushing bride is. *Oui!* It is, *vous*, *Contessa*! Yes! You, *Contessa*! Now what, I ask myself, is the *Contesse de Le Touquet*'s wedding photograph doing in Diane Barker's bag in the back of the stolen car?

Reaper (*slapping his thigh*) I've got it! I've got it! How stupid of me. It *is* your bag, *Contesse*. Don't you recognize it?

Mrs Barker tries to nod

You must have left it in the back of the car on some *previous* occasion. Days ago, perhaps.

Ruff Aha! The initials "D.B."?

Reaper Du Bonnet. Genevieve Du Bonnet. You remember, Genevieve gave it to you at that ball in Deauville, remember? You admired her bag and she pressed it upon you. (*To Ruff*) Genevieve's like that. Gives everything away that anyone takes a fancy to.

Ruff I'd like to meet Genevieve one day.

Reaper takes the locket, looks at it, and laughs fondly

Reaper Charming. Lovely likeness. You and the *Comte*.
Ruff *That* is the *Comte de Le Touquet*, sir?
Reaper That's right.
Ruff This shaven-haired gentleman with the cauliflower ears and broken nose? To me it looks like a British all-in wrestler known as the Bosham Strangler. Real name Jim Barker. Married to a girl called Diane.
Reaper Does it really? (*To Mrs Barker*) *Quel coincidence. Très amusant.* (*To Ruff*) I'm just explaining to her. (*To Mrs Barker, with a loud laugh*) You'll have a laugh when you tell Jean Pierre on your return to Le Touquet.
Ruff Boulogne, sir.
Reaper Pardon?
Ruff The *Contesse de Le Touquet* lives in Boulogne, or so you told me.
Reaper Yes, but she always travels back via Le Touquet.
Ruff Why?
Reaper Sentimental reasons. People stand in the streets to wave at her.
Ruff Well, they would, wouldn't they? Lady Godiva all over again.
Reaper If that's all, Inspector . . . ?
Ruff (*exploding*) ALL! ALL! If you think I'm going to accept that load of codswallop you've got another think coming!

In the kitchen a cloud of black smoke starts to pour out of the closed oven

Reaper Are you suggesting that we are liars?
Ruff I'm not suggesting. I'm telling you *flat*. And I've enough evidence now to ask you to accompany me to the station to make a signed statement . . .
Reaper You have no evidence of anything. I demand to see my lawyer.
Ruff You can see all the lawyers you like, but . . . (*He stops, sniffs*)

Smoke billows out of the oven

Something burning. In there.
Reaper (*in horror*) No! Oh, no!

Ruff hurries into the kitchen. Reaper, realizing the worst, hastens after him, trying to impede him. Mrs Barker sinks, defeated, on to the sofa. Fogg rushes off in the opposite direction and runs into the bedroom, closing the connecting door after him. (The ensuing scene in the kitchen and bedroom must be carefully staged so that one does not interfere with the other.) In the bedroom: Fogg goes straight to Reaper's trousers and starts a frantic search for the money in Reaper's discarded clothes. He finds it. In the kitchen: Ruff heads to the stove, Reaper tries to stop him

Don't open that. I'm cooking something.
Ruff You have been all the evening. Out of my way!

Reaper, now defeated, leans back against the door as Ruff opens the oven and starts to fish out the contents, with difficulty. In the bedroom, Fogg runs to the bathroom door and knocks

Diane looks out

Fogg Listen, there's no need to give you the money.

Diane Why?

Fogg Eddie knows about those nude pictures and doesn't care. So just get home before he does and you're safe.

Diane Can't. I've dropped my key somewhere in the bathroom.

Fogg If Eddie doesn't murder you, I will. Find it and get out.

Diane disappears back inside the bathroom. Fogg slams the bathroom door, rushes across the room, through the connecting door, and exits through the shop door

Mrs Barker watches him go with interest. She rises and goes into the bedroom. She reacts in surprise as there comes a thin, sad wailing noise from the bathroom. Meanwhile, in the kitchen, hampered by heat and smoke, Ruff removes the following items from the oven: the remains of two pies, and the partially burnt remains of Mrs Barker's shirt and slacks

Ruff Now what have we here? Remains of a pie. Not much future in that, I'd say. You probably have not much appetite by now, anyway, sir? But this other stuff looks much more interesting.

Reaper moves away and enters the sitting-room. Mrs Barker returns to the sitting-room at the same time

Reaper It's no use. He's found your clothes. I put them in the oven. Didn't know the blasted thing was turned on.

Mrs Barker That's it, then. By the way, she's still hiding here, too.

Reaper Who?

Mrs Barker Eddie Reaper's wife. She hasn't gone. She's in the bathroom crying.

Reaper What! (*He makes a move towards the bedroom*)

Ruff comes out of the kitchen carrying the clothes, which he puts on a table

Ruff No proof, eh, sir? May I present the remains of one much sought-after striped shirt and one pair of blue lady's slacks.

Reaper My goodness!

Ruff You sound surprised, sir.

Reaper Who, me?

Ruff Yes, you. You said you were cooking them.

Reaper When?

Ruff Just now.

Reaper Who, me?

Ruff Yes, you!

Reaper Not them. The *pies*. It was—my partner. He cooks clothes. He must have put them there. Where is he? (*He glares towards the bedroom*)

Fogg, breathless, enters through the shop door

Ruff Here he is! Where have you been, sir?

Fogg Putting the money back in the—locking—the shop—oven—door . . .

Ruff I see. Well, in your absence we've made a little discovery in the shape of the missing shirt and slacks.

Reaper Yes! Explain yourself.

Ruff comes across something in the pocket of the slacks. He fishes it out

Ruff Wait a minute! (*He brings out the stone parcel*) Look at this! Here's something. A little scorched, perhaps, but luckily diamonds don't burn, do they? (*To them all, grimly*) Gotcha!

Reaper I must say, I am shocked! Shocked! (*To Fogg*) I think it's time you came clean, you stinker!

Fogg (*calmly*) Very well, if you insist.

Ruff He does insist. We all do.

Fogg Right. (*To Mrs Barker*) For a start, I'm Roger Fogg and he is Eddie Reaper.

Mrs Barker Huh?

Ruff (*impatiently*) We know that, sir . . .

Fogg Correction. *She* doesn't. She thinks I'm Reaper and he's Fogg.

Reaper This has nothing to do——

Ruff ⎱
Fogg ⎰ (*cutting in*) Shut up! ⎱ (*Speaking together*)

Fogg I wasn't driving my car tonight. He borrowed it. To take her out. He's been borrowing my name, too, because he's a married man.

Reaper You—you—*thing!*

Fogg You told me to come clean.

Reaper Not as clean as that!

Mrs Barker suddenly grabs Reaper and pulls him close

Mrs Barker You are Eddie Reaper?

Reaper Well, yes and no. We have an agreement in the partnership which enables us to borrow each other's name.

Mrs Barker clouts Reaper hard with her handbag. He falls into a chair

Mrs Barker Ooh, stuff it!

Ruff What's that French for?

Fogg *Pâté de fois gras.*

Mrs Barker bursts into tears, snatches the clothes from the table, and exits through the front door

Reaper (*groaning, gasping*) Assault and battery! Stop her!

Ruff (*enjoying it*) No. She won't get anywhere. I've a man on the door, and I must ask you two gentlemen to accompany me to the station where you and Mrs Barker will be formally charged with harbouring a quantity of diamonds stolen from a person or persons unknown.

Fogg Before you go, Inspector. I'd like to report the theft from the person or persons unknown. I know who they are.

Ruff Who?

Fogg Us. Him and me. Reaper and Fogg. The diamonds came from our shop. I've just discovered. Our main safe was broken into some time tonight.

Reaper But the alarm didn't go off.

Fogg Your fault. You didn't lock up properly when you went out earlier to pick the girl up. They must have got in then.

Ruff What did they take?

Fogg (*triumphantly*) One stone parcel containing forty-five diamonds.

Ruff holds up the bag and begins to mouth something

Yes! You'll find forty in there, and the five you've got which were found in my car makes up the lot. Thanks very much, Inspector.

Ruff B-b-but this means . . . (*He removes the other diamonds from his pocket*)

Fogg It means you can't very well charge us with stealing our own property.

Ruff is twitching himself now

In fact, you can't charge me with anything at all.

Ruff Oooh! (*Defeated, he bangs the parcel and diamonds down on a table. This causes him to see something—Fogg's log-book. He seizes it, waves it with a crazed look in his eye*) Oh yes, I can. There's the little matter of smooth tyres, no insurance, no road fund licence, and no MOT.

Reaper Ha! Ha! Yes! Good work, Inspector! Nick him!

Ruff Nick him? I'd like to nick you too, sir, but we must be thankful for small mercies. (*To Fogg*) Remember, Mr Fogg, pride comes before a fall.

Ruff hurls the log-book down, permits himself a triumphant if slightly crazed little giggle, and exits through the front door

This is followed by a cry and a series of descending thumps as of a heavy man falling down a flight of stairs. Fogg looks at Reaper and tries a smile

Fogg It could have been worse.

Reaper utters a dangerously friendly laugh

Well, at least that girl's husband and your wife won't find out what's happened.

Reaper I'm glad you're worried about my wife. *I'm* worried about her, too. She must be feeling very lonely.

Fogg Then why not go to her?

Reaper Just what I propose to do. Out of my way, Fogg, and prepare to meet thy doom.

Fogg desperately intercepts him

Fogg Wait! I can explain everything. (*He bars Reaper*)

Reaper Stand back. The axe is about to fall.

Reaper hurls Fogg aside and starts his final charge towards the bedroom door

Simultaneously Ruff enters through the front door

Ruff and Reaper collide

Out of my way.

Ruff (*grabbing Reaper*) Wait! Mr Reaper, *I* now have a confession to make.

Reaper What?

Ruff Downstairs just now I fell into the *Contesse*. She was in a highly hysterical state. She asked for your home address and, like a fool, I gave it to her.

Reaper (*frozen*) You—gave—her—my home address?

Ruff Yes. That was when I realized I had made a booboo. She said something about going to tell your missus everything, then confess to her husband . . .

Reaper He'll murder me!

Ruff (*giggling wildly*) Yes, that's what she said.

Reaper Stop her!

Ruff (*barring him*) Too late. I let her go. Saw her into a taxi. Even paid her fare.

Ruff's eyes meet Reaper's eyes, and a slow, triumphant smile takes over from Ruff's pseudo-apologetic expression

Ruff, suppressing a delighted giggle, exits through the front door

Reaper (*pleasantly*) Oh well. I suppose it could be worse.

Fogg (*surprised*) It could?

Reaper Yes, I might have had a heart attack before I strangled you; then, again, she won't find my wife at home.

Fogg Oh?

Reaper No, because she's *still hiding in your bathroom.*

Fogg No!

Diane comes out of the bathroom wearing Fogg's sweater and jeans. She exits through the window

Reaper grabs at Fogg. The front door buzzer sounds. Fogg answers it, pressing the button

Help! Help!

A girl's voice, with a foreign accent, comes over the intercom

Girl's Voice Is Mr Fogg there?

Fogg Yes. Who wants him?

Girl's Voice It is his wife, Juliana Fogg, from Amsterdam.

Fogg Wife . . . ! Amsterdam? I haven't . . .

Girl's Voice Foggee—Foggee—is that you? I have some wonderful **news** for you! Can you guess my *little* surprise?

Fogg advances on Reaper

Fogg You've been at it again! Haven't you? Now I'm going to have a baby!

With a bellow of rage Fogg chases Reaper, as—

the CURTAIN *falls*

FURNITURE AND PROPERTY LIST

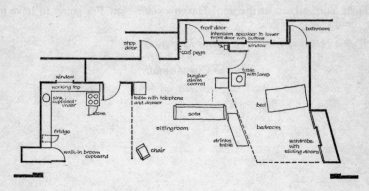

ACT I

On stage: SITTING-ROOM:

Sofa. *On it:* cushions

Armchair

Drinks table with assorted bottles, including whisky, water-jug with water, glasses

Table with drawer. *On it:* telephone. *In drawer:* car log-book, insurance, MOT, roll of black cotton with loop at end, torch

On walls: burglar alarm control board and instruction pamphlet, intercom by bedroom door with button, coat-pegs

BEDROOM:

Table. *On it:* lamp

Bed with fitted sheet, pillow and case, duvet, concealed duplicate bath-towel. (*This is a special bed with recess*)

Built-in wardrobe cupboard. *In it:* 2 shirts, dressing-gown, 3 pairs of similar trousers, slip-on man's shoes

On walls: alarm bell, pictures

Window curtains

KITCHEN:

Electric cooker

Refrigerator. *In it:* milk, cheese, etc.

Shelves with food, tins, salt, plastic drinking glass

Working top. *On it:* large tureen, special divided saucepan, wooden spoon. *In drawer:* rolling-pin

Sink with one practical tap. *In cupboard below:* bucket

Walk-in broom cupboard

Hanger on swivel above cooker

BATHROOM:

Shelf with bathroom equipment, lotions, etc.

Off stage: 2 meat pies, tin of baked beans **(Fogg)**
            Wet umbrella **(Fogg)**
            Imitation cat **(Fogg)**
            Cigar stub **(Reaper)**
            Wet umbrella **(Reaper)**
            Nudie magazine **(Diane)**
            Wad of banknotes **(Fogg)**
            Bottle of champagne **(Reaper)**
            Small bath-towel **(Diane)**
            Diamond packet with diamonds **(Mrs Barker)**
            Set behind electric stove: materials for smoke effect; set of burned
               black clothes to match Diane's; packet of puffed wheat and gun
               (for explosion)

Personal: **Fogg:** 2 sets of keys, wad of banknotes
            Reaper: 1 set of keys, jeweller's eyeglass, pocket calculator, visiting-
              card, pair of tweezers
            Ruff: walkie-talkie radio, identity card, notepad, pen, loose diamonds

ACT II

Off stage: Small hand-towel **(Mrs Barker)**
            Spare key **(Fogg)**
            Lady's handbag with initials D.B. containing nightie and gold locket
               (Ruff)
            Set behind electric stove: 2 burnt pies; set of burned clothes to match
               Mrs Barker's with scorched diamond packet in pocket

EFFECT OF THE EXPLODING BEAN TIN

This effect was achieved in the West End production by the following method:
One hotplate on the electric stove was "doctored" to take a tube which was attached to a cylinder of compressed air. The saucepan into which the baked bean tin was placed was divided into three compartments. One section took the tin, the second section the water used to heat up the tin, whilst the third section had its base removed and replaced by a fine-mesh grille. On top of this grille was placed puffed wheat and the whole saucepan was set on the hotplate with the third section over the tube leading to the compressed air. To cause the "explosion" a gun was fired for the noise and compressed air was applied to the puffed wheat to cause the visual effect.

LIGHTING PLOT

Property fittings required: wall brackets, kitchen pendant, bedroom pendant, bedroom table lamp with 2 circular glass shades, specially rigged electric cooker with four rings which light up and glow when switched on, flashing lights on burglar alarm (not essential)

Interior. A flat. The same scene throughout

ACT I Evening

To open: Kitchen and sitting-room lights on; bedroom in darkness

Cue 1	**Fogg** turns off sitting-room lights	(Page 2)
	Snap off brackets and covering lights	
Cue 2	**Ruff** switches on bedroom lights	(Page 2)
	Snap on bedroom pendant and covering lights	
Cue 3	**Fogg** switches on sitting-room lights	(Page 3)
	Snap on wall brackets and covering lights	
Cue 4	**Fogg** switches on one electric ring	(Page 5)
	Bring up glow on electric ring	
Cue 5	**Diane** switches on remaining three rings	(Page 9)
	Bring up glow on three electric rings	
Cue 6	**Fogg** switches off all electric rings	(Page 16)
	Quick fade of all electric rings	

ACT II Evening

To open: As close of Act I

Cue 7	**Fogg** switches on four electric rings	(Page 36)
	Bring up glow on four rings	
Cue 8	**Diane** switches off electric rings	(Page 40)
	Fade all electric rings	
Cue 9	**Mrs Barker** switches on four electric rings	(Page 45)
	Bring up glow on four rings	
Cue 10	**Reaper** switches off four electric rings	(Page 46)
	Fade all electric rings	

EFFECTS PLOT

ACT I

Cue 1	On rise of CURTAIN *Sound of heavy rain, gradually fading*	(Page 1)
Cue 2	Shortly after rise of CURTAIN *Burglar alarm bell*	(Page 1)
Cue 3	During sound of burglar alarm *Sound of approaching footsteps on wood*	(Page 1)
Cue 4	Fogg: ". . . Switch One." *Loud buzzer*	(Page 1)
Cue 5	Fogg: ". . . ultra-sonic protection." *High-pitched noise*	(Page 2)
Cue 6	Fogg: ". . . floor-pads." *Burglar alarm bell*	(Page 2)
Cue 7	Fogg: ". . . warning buzzer." *Beeping buzzer*	(Page 2)
Cue 8	After cessation of beeping buzzer *Noise outside bedroom window*	(Page 2)
Cue 9	Fogg: "There's no Sweetie . . ." *Front door buzzer*	(Page 7)
Cue 10	Diane: "What's up?" *Cloud of smoke from opened oven*	(Page 15)
Cue 11	Fogg: "Good night." *Front door buzzer*	(Page 16)
Cue 12	Fogg: ". . . blonde with arthritis." *Burglar alarm bell*	(Page 24)
Cue 13	Reaper: ". . . the room had no bed . . ." *Explosion of baked beans tin*	(Page 26)
Cue 14	Fogg: "You shock me altogether." *Crashing sounds from kitchen broom cupboard*	(Page 29)
Cue 15	Reaper: ". . . what a dull life I lead." *Front door buzzer*	(Page 32)

ACT II

Cue 16	Reaper turns on electric rings *Front door buzzer*	(Page 36)
Cue 17	Reaper extracts imaginary fly from Ruff's foot *Burglar alarm bell*	(Page 39)
Cue 18	Diane exits through bedroom window *Burglar alarm bell*	(*Page* 41)

Cue 19   **Fogg:** "We've had it."   (Page 44)
          Sound of heavy rain

Cue 20   **Fogg** in bedroom pulls cotton reel   (Page 47)
          Burglar alarm bell. Rain sound fades

Cue 21   **Ruff:** ". . . and maybe some cash."   (Page 53)
          Tinny voice on police radio

Cue 22   **Ruff:** "Ruff here. Over."   (Page 53)
          Tinny voice on police radio

Cue 23   **Ruff:** ". . . you've got another think coming!" (Page 58)
          Smoke seeps out of closed oven

Cue 24   **Ruff:** "Out of my way!"   (Page 58)
          Smoke pours out of open oven

Cue 25   **Ruff:** ". . . pride comes before a fall."   (Page 61)
          After Ruff's exit, sound of heavy body falling downstairs,
          *   followed by a cry*

Cue 26   **Fogg:** "No!"   (Page 62)
          Front door buzzer